THE TERMINATION TRAP

BEST STRATEGIES FOR A JOB GOING SOUR

BY

Stephen Cohen, M.D.

Illustrations by Alex Tiani

WILLIAMSON PUBLISHING CO.

CHURCH HILL ROAD, CHARLOTTE, VERMONT 05445

Copyright © 1984 by Stephen Cohen, M.D.

All rights reserved. No portion of this book may be reproduced—mechanically, electronically or by any other means, including photocopying—without written permission of the publisher.

Library of Congress Cataloging in Publication Data
Cohen, Stephen, 1941-
   The termination trap.
   1. Employees, Resignation of. 2. Employees, Dismissal of.
   I. Title.
HF5549.5.R54C63   1984   650.1   83-26087
ISBN 0-913589-00-4 (pbk.)

Cover and interior design: Trezzo-Braren Studio
Illustrations: Alex Tiani
Printing: Capital City Press

Williamson Publishing
Charlotte, Vermont 05445

Manufactured in the United States of America

First printing March 1984

CONTENTS

PREFACE _____ 5

INTRODUCTION _____ 9

1 WHO SETS THE TERMINATION TRAP?
ME, YOU, OR THEM _____ 15

2 A PERSONAL CHECKLIST
IS THERE A TRAP LURKING IN YOUR FUTURE? ____ 21

3 HOW ORGANIZATIONS WORK
ARE TRAPS PART OF THE STRUCTURE? _____ 35

4 SAVING YOUR JOB FROM SET-UPS
THE TRAPS YOU CAN MANEUVER AROUND _____ 57

5 GIVING YOURSELF A CHANCE
PERSONAL STRESSES YOU CAN MANAGE NOW ___ 109

6 GOING OUT EASY
RECOGNIZING PUSH-OUTS, THE ONE-WAY TRAPS __ 117

7 WIN, LOSE, OR DRAW
SURVIVING A SET-UP OR PUSH-OUT _____ 157

8 TODAY I LOST MY JOB
WHEN THE TRAP SNAPS SHUT _____ 173

9 BOUNCING OFF THE WALLS AT WORK AND HOME
FINAL RESPONSES TO BEING SNARED _____ 189

10 THE EMOTIONAL AFTERMATH
COMING TO TERMS WITH YOURSELF _____ 199

11 A BOUNCER IN SHARKSKIN
A HELPING HAND FOR WHOSE BENEFIT? _____ 213

12 LIFE AFTER JOB LOSS
A REVIEW _____ 221

READING LIST _____ 223

THE CORNER OFFICE

To place him in the corner office was an act of vengeance
because he didn't belong there. Trying his entire life
to adjust to a set of immovable circumstances,

he sold a lot of leases but could never sell himself.
There was something he couldn't project because he couldn't
demonstrate he had talent. A gaping hole

he tried to fill with little infidelities
and although he was nice he was confused enough
to hurt some people. We gave him the corner office

and he could sit there and look out two sets of windows
and tally up his stock options and count the time
until the whole thing caught up with him

and he would be forced ineluctably out of the company,
never knowing how he had been handled
nor suspecting how much some people knew.

—Richard Grossman
from *Tycoon Boy*

PREFACE

The hero of the 1936 Olympics, Jesse Owens, gave me my first lesson in handling the problem of a job going sour. It was 1953. I was a teen-aged caddy at Sunset Ridge Golf course, the only public course in a suburb of twenty-five thousand north of Chicago. The other five courses were private clubs. Mr. Owens' black skin and my parents' lower middle class status brought us together at Sunset Ridge. One day I was caddying in his foursome where the men were playing for a lot more money than I was to be paid. The bag I was carrying had a double set of irons and two extra woods. It outweighed me by at least ten pounds, and the temperature was above ninety. My golfer, a competitive Caucasian conservative, Mr. K., was losing to Mr. Owens by three strokes at the end of the sixth hole. I was losing to the heat and the heaviness of the bag.

I dropped the red and white golf bag accidentally, just as Mr. K. teed off on the seventh. The noise was nowhere near as deafening as his yelling at me. I was too dry to produce tears, and my defensive excuses caught in my throat.

Two greens later, Mr. K. was two more strokes down and I was starting to drag the new leather golf bag. He angrily suggested that I run ahead and rent him a pullcart. "I'll make it," I told him. Three dollars was a lot of money to me. He asked if any of my friends could pick up for me at the end of the ninth hole. I told him no. Then he asked if I were sick. "No, I don't think so," I stiffened with the tension. "Stephen, my boy, you are a gentleman and a scholar. This is not your kind of work." I told him I enjoyed caddying, besides I was saving up for college. He told me that he had a future, too. He was planning to buy his own pullcart. I remember feeling a knot in my stomach. Then he turned to Mr. Owens and said, "You know, Jesse (I don't remember his ever using Mr. Owens' name before), I think having a caddy is slowing down my game."

On the ninth green I removed the final ball from the cup and handed it to Mr. K. "Don't bother washing it," he said. I was surprised, he was a stickler for clean balls. "Run to the clubhouse, will you, and rent me a cart."

Too wilted to argue, I asked him for the money. Then the famous Jesse Owens asked if he could join me. He said he was going to get a soda. On the way he asked me if I had ever been fired. I told him no. He then told me to get prepared for it. Mr. K. was pretty upset about losing money and was taking it out on me. Mr. Owens also suggested that next time I do a better job of sizing up the golf bag I was being asked to carry. Lastly, he bought me a soda and told me to be careful that I got paid what was due me.

Back on the tenth tee I was prepared to carry on with the golf cart as my new assistant. Mr. K. asked me for change. I told him that he owed me fifty cents; he hadn't given me enough money for the cart. Then he handed me one and a half dollars. "This is for the nine holes, I'll use the cart. Put the bag on the cart."

I was puzzled, although somewhat prepared. "But, usually a caddy gets a dollar fifty plus tip for nine holes," I responded.

"Sorry," he said, "you did a lousy job."

"I did, but you hired me to do it. You only paid me one dollar. I paid for part of your cart."

"That's for the inconvenience," he said.

"Listen," I said, "this isn't fair."

"You're fired, son," he smiled coldly at me, "now leave, or I'll be sure you never caddy here again."

Mr. Owens stepped forward and put his hand on my shoulder. Looking over toward Mr. K. he gave me a dollar. "I'll be winning more of this stuff from Mr. K. on the next nine holes." He winked at me. Some consolation, but not as much as what happened three weeks later when Mr. K. asked me to caddy for him again. It seemed that he had become tired of pulling his own cart.

With Jesse Owens' prior support hidden deep inside me, I told him that I would, providing he paid me two dollars for nine holes and four fifty for eighteen. I was the only person in the caddy shack at the time. We also struck a bargain on the number of clubs he would carry in his golf bag. I had learned my lesson.

This book is about those dynamic, complex forces at work which can disrupt your job. I have emphasized how to observe what is happening to you when your job goes sour, then understand the underlying forces, and lastly, develop a set of coping behaviors. The book is intended to be used as a guideline for developing valuable skills to help you keep your job in the face of destructive forces or to cope with being fired.

Working as a psychiatrist means I am at great risk for speaking psycho-babble, and its more scientific off-shoots, medicalese and psychiatrese. In an effort to avoid this, I also risk oversimplification of complex subjects. I have tried to walk this tightrope by using humor and metaphors to lighten the load. I don't want to create a shallow primer; I also don't want to tire out people who are already undergoing stress. I have made specific suggestions throughout this book. It is not that these are the only ways to handle specific problems. The main goal is to help you remain in control of your work-life. The true pain of the threat, or the event, of a soured job (and the possibility of getting fired) is bewilderment and immobility. My intent is to offer hope through practical suggestions to help others get "unstuck" and back to controlling their own work-life.

The ideas discussed in this book were harvested from fifteen years of interest in group and corporate activity; organizational consultations; psychotherapy with firing and fired individuals; interviews with employers, "outplacement professionals," and fired employees; and my own work experience.

The events portrayed in this book have been slightly altered to protect the innocent and the guilty. Many of the stories were related during that especially confidential time called psychotherapy. These episodes have been more carefully altered to hide any recognition of people and situations.

I want to thank Susan Williamson for her initial idea for this book and her subsequent editorial help. Others who have been of direct or indirect assistance are Jonathan Leopold, Andrea Chesman, Ken Braren, Kenneth Artiss, Eric Miller, Kenneth Rice, Seymour Perlin, Joel Elkes, Jack Mulholland, Charles Jenkins, Jack Williamson, and of course, Trudi, Adam, and David.

For Bill Cohen:
He showed me that
hard work
can get done with
fairness, concern, and
love

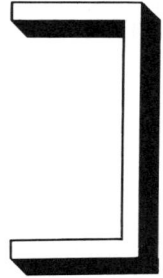

INTRODUCTION

We have all experienced it; maybe not personally, but we've all seen someone suddenly (at least it *seemed* sudden) out of work. It may have been a friend, relative, neighbor, or someone in another department at the office; it may have been you. The word gets out that Joe X. or Mary S. quit in a huff, or resigned, or took early retirement, or decided to take an extended leave of absence. Whatever they called it, the experience was likely the same. One day they were at work; the next day they were gone for good.

It's almost as if the person died; here today, gone tomorrow. Maybe that's why we tend not to talk about it; sort of like having a miscarriage—no one knows what to say. One thing's for sure, when anyone is fired for whatever reasons, we feel a gnawing vulnerability that we may be next. And in this age of high tech, we may even begin to feel more than vulnerable; we feel that it is *inevitable* that sooner or later we, too, will fall victim to a Termination Trap.

But losing a job doesn't have to happen. It's not part of the natural course of events; in fact, it *feels* very unnatural, and the discomfort it causes serves as ample warning to those sensitized to maneuver around the trap. Yes, with proper skills, you can not only avoid the Termination Trap, but actually take control of your work-life.

■ If you presently have a job you like, then here are some important *job-keeping* skills you need to learn now.

■ If you already feel trapped at work, then here are some *job-saving* skills you need to apply immediately.

■ If you have just lost your job, then here are some *job-leaving* skills you'll want to use immediately.

■ If you've already experienced termination for whatever reason, then here are some very necessary *coping* skills you'll use now and long after you begin working again.

How are you going to accomplish all of this? It's not easy but it is definitely possible. This book can help you:

■ Locate the sources of the early-warning feelings of being trapped

■ Analyze the ways these sources operate to lure you into the trap

■ Save and improve your job (if this is feasible and desirable) or

■ Leave the job for whatever reason with your professional, personal, and emotional lives intact

■ Learn enough about yourself and the nature of the workplace to better cope with any work environment

If you have been terminated already, and you are still feeling the painful reverberations of the wounds, this book can help you:

■ Review and understand what happened to you

■ Consider changes (personal, attitudinal, and practical) that will enhance your chances for successful employment in the future

■ Sort through and relieve the complex feelings that can seem so painful and sticky right now

■ Learn enough about yourself and the nature of the workplace to better cope with any future work environment

No matter what your present work status is, I want to stimulate your thinking about what is happening to you, to help you to develop skills in observation, and to learn how to take these observations and apply them to your particular circumstances. This book should increase your ability to study yourself and your work environment.

SOME PREMISES
TO CONSIDER

In order to get the most out of this book, I have to ask you to accept certain ideas.

PEOPLE DON'T OFTEN SAY
WHAT THEY REALLY THINK;
THEREFORE, ACTIONS
SPEAK LOUDER THAN WORDS.

I hope you can accept the proposition that few people say in words what they really feel and mean. This becomes more obvious the harder it is to express something. Yet, if you are willing to look closely, it is possible to perceive what another person's inner feelings and thoughts are. Begin now to develop those skills which will be very helpful to you on the job, as well as in your home life. The overall goal is to broaden your level of awareness beyond the actual words, so that you can ferret out the *intended* messages. Here's how to do it.

Examine People's Behavior. What about their eyebrows, lip muscles, body posture, voice inflection, and the myriad other nonverbal cues? Look for discrepancies between what is being said and the nonverbal messages you are receiving.

Examine Your Responses to What Is Happening. Your responses are often valid clues, especially when you notice that your response to a particular occurrence is not a usual response for you. Isn't it true that intuition is a response uncontaminated by outside bias and can be a very good indicator of what is happening? How many times have you "kicked yourself" because you felt something was going to happen, but distrusted your feeling and did nothing about it?

Examine the Context of Management's Statements. When do the statements occur? How do the statements relate to what was said, or done, just previous to their being stated? Who is making the statements, and what authority and responsibility do they have?

Examine Every Office Memo. These are formal records documenting the process of communication in your company. Keep all memos. Every now and then read them in chronological order. The evolution of formal communications (as shown in the memos) will often tell you a lot about what is going to happen.

An uncomfortable example of how the process and timing of a memo can be a valuable clue to what is going to happen occurred during the Johnson administration. It became national headline news that a Russian trawler had bumped an American naval vessel in the Gulf of Tonkin (near Vietnam). One might have wondered what this "memo" was all about. It was (and still is) common knowledge that Russian and American vessels track one another so closely everywhere in the world that these bumpings and harassments occur frequently. Why was this one a headline? A few weeks later came Johnson's Tonkin Resolution and the beginning of our formal involvement in Vietnam. It would appear as if the White House and the military were using the news media's hunger for press releases to heat up the American public's anti-North Vietnam feelings.

Examine the Nature of the Informal Groupings at Work. Isn't it important who lunches or plays tennis with whom? Isn't it important who an executive secretary has as close personal friends at work?

It is important to learn to make these kinds of observations. In order to find the Termination Trap you have to be able to read the signals correctly. Once you have begun the process of making observations, some sense has to be made of them. For this we need a second premise.

THE WHOLE IS GREATER
THAN THE SUM OF ITS PARTS.

When people interact in groups, and when groups interact with other groups, the attitudes, beliefs, and morals that are expressed are something other than just the sum of the individuals making up the group. I am not saying that companies have personalities. But leadership does have a style of managing that influences every aspect of conducting business within any organization. This includes everything from making and enforcing major corporate decisions to influencing the atmosphere in the cafeteria. The leadership style provides the ambience for a company. That is why nothing feels the same after a company changes hands, even when everyone keeps their same jobs. The following is an example of how the whole of a company is greater than the sum of its individual parts.

A large midwestern corporation printed religious books filled with love, God, holiness, truth, goodness, honesty, and striving to do good things for one's fellow man. Most employees saw themselves and their work guided by religious traditions. Though the company had grown considerably, the president continued to run it like "the good old days." He could not delegate authority because of a very private fear that someone else's mistake would cause him to lose financial security.

This management style worked well for many years, but a time came when the company outgrew the president's capacity to monitor all of its functions. Eventually he hired six bright, energetic young men as managers. They were carefully instructed to report to him individually. There were never any group meetings. He listened to their ideas, made his own suggestions, and the company continued to prosper financially.

One or two top level managers either quit or were squeezed out each year. The president's wife found the departures painful and sudden. It became evident that the six managers were spending a lot of time competing with one another for the president's attention and favor. All decisions were made in private with him. Many decisions were unilaterally rescinded by the president without his consulting anyone. Most employees felt that whatever happened behind closed doors was totally secret. People felt they had to go to the president, present the problem or issue, and then hope the president would handle it by talking with someone else.

The president's need to control everything resulted in six managers unable, and then unwilling, to get along. Competition, backstabbing, rumors, and increased sick leave time became rampant. The employees blamed one another and their managers for the stress. The managers began using the president's closed door to convey dissatisfaction with their peers. The turnover in this group of six people accelerated. It took seven years of chaos for the president to wonder if he were doing something wrong.

This is a clear example of how an administrative style bloomed from just one person. This doesn't happen just in privately held companies. It can occur in any work situation where a boss has enough authority, or support from above, to personalize the work environment. In this example, the owner's insecurity and his own need to control everything resulted in secretiveness, distrust, competitiveness among employees, and employee turnover and attrition. There was no one in this Bible printing company who would describe himself as secretive, untrustworthy, competitive, or hateful. The whole was different from the sum of its parts.

By accepting these few premises and sharpening your perception skills, you will be more able to use the many coping behaviors suggested throughout this book. Understanding what is happening to you will make it easier to adopt more personal trap-less solutions for yourself. Developing these new skills will also serve you when searching for a new job. Knowing how to find potential traps before taking a job gives you the opportunity for mastering their intricacies, or possibly avoiding them (and maybe even the job) altogether.

1

WHO SETS THE TERMINATION TRAP? ME, YOU, OR THEM

There are many ways to get forced out of a job. You might get terminated for inadequate job performance on a reasonable, assigned task. Maybe you willingly (and naively) undertook an impossible job and then suffered the consequences of failing to accomplish it. Maybe you were terminated for doing a job well that could, and should, have been done. This is a romantic termination: the employee who fulfills the mission of the job, but somehow isn't appreciated. An even more heroic and romantic Termination Trap is getting fired for doing a job well that nobody felt actually could be done. Maybe you got trapped by other factors less under your control. Certainly it could have been management's fault. We all have that inclination to see other's flaws before our own, so let's begin with those traps set by others.

You can be Set-Up to lose your job or you can be Pushed-Out. The Set-Up allows you more room to maneuver back into your job, but is also more subtle and therefore harder to ferret out, understand, and respond to. The Push-Out is closer to being irreversible, but it's more easily recognizable. The advantage of a Push-Out is that you can begin interacting more quickly, so you tend to feel more involved and goal-oriented, less helpless, and less victimized. Push-Outs are still painful.

Ownership and management are not inherently evil or dangerous. Our bosses do not get up in the mornings, look in their mirrors, sharpen their canine teeth into points, grimace, and say, "I wonder what evil I can do today."

Many times it seems right to remove people from work because they are not doing what they were hired to do, for whatever reasons. While the law protects your right to *not* work, it also protects your company's right to fire you without reason (if you are not under contract). Courts are willing to support a company which fires an employee with a contract, if it can be shown that the employee exhibited behaviors that are morally unfit for reasons of dishonesty, immorality, socially deviant behavior, intoxication, negligence, incompetence, or unresponsiveness to authority.

So the fear of a company's power to fire is soundly based in reality. There is something very dark and ominous about the power of management to take away your job without you having any say in the matter. This can happen whether or not you were doing your job very well. It does not matter in this book if the job soured, or was lost, for "right" or "wrong" reasons. The same things occur to the person getting fired for "good" reasons as occur to the person getting fired for "bad" or "unfair" reasons. A job in trouble is filled with many chances for getting caught in the Termination Trap. Often employees walk uninvited into the traps, and sometimes even set their own traps for getting fired.

Getting caught unaware in a trap—a set of actions which can result in you losing your job—can happen for many reasons. It is quite easy to get caught given how much trouble well-intentioned people have communicating. Usually, most people communicate indirectly, especially if the message is uncomfortable to them or negative to another person. This indirectness is what makes the atmosphere surrounding a job going sour so much like a trap. If you can not read the indirect signals, then you don't know where the trap is, how it is baited, or when you might fall into it. This often creates a vague feeling of uneasiness, which clouds your perceptions and decisions as you walk through the day-to-day decisions and actions of your job. People and institutions do say what they really mean, but rarely directly. There are, however, little events if you are sensitized to them, which signal what is to happen.

Let's begin a journey to understand the indirect communications that take place at work when someone is about to be fired. With that understanding, you will regain control of your work-life, and be able to make the decisions necessary to save your job or to leave in your own style. You can take positive, constructive steps to maximize control of your own destiny the entire way.

ORGANIZATIONS DON'T LIKE
TO FIRE PEOPLE

It's hard to fire someone these days. Remember that. For your employer, firing can involve time-consuming details which take away from getting other work done. There often has to be a formal submission of evidence of malperformance at work, the drudgery of keeping adequate records to substantiate this evidence against you, and (in the case of large corporations or the federal government) the establishment of independent investigative bodies with your right to cross-examine. This potential for legal backfire makes firing a direct assault on the company as well as the employee. Managers run the risk of exposing their own failures and that of the organization during the cross-examinations that can occur in formal firing procedures. There is a potential threat to the image of the corporation and the manager as humane, hardworking, rational, and honest. Also, dismissing an employee can be disruptive to those employees left behind.

There are still more roadblocks. Threats of litigation, concern for providing nonthreatening employment for those employees not getting fired, and fears of unionization or office walkouts, all put pressure on management to avoid firing if possible.

Your boss may feel very uncomfortable when firing you. So the person doing the firing feels uncomfortable. So what? Well something has to be done with all the discomfort: the guilt of turning a person away from his or her livelihood; the shame of possibly making a mistake when deciding to push out, or fire, someone; the anxiety of inflicting pain on someone; and the fears of what might happen to the employee when told to leave the workplace. (Will there be a heart attack or suicide, leaving blood on my hands? Will I be attacked, or killed, leaving my blood on his hands? Will company secrets be stolen by a disgruntled fired employee? These are a few common fears of bosses doing the firing.) Their discomfort goes away when they take the path of least resistance.

Your boss, without evil intent, begins to behave in such a way that he or she can fire you with minimal discomfort. And all of this is done without anyone necessarily plotting against you.

No wonder your early discomfort feels so vague; the person doing the firing hasn't even acquired the self-knowledge of what he or she has, in fact, already begun to do.

There are ways for companies to get rid of unwanted employees and avoid the pain and embarrassment for themselves. That's where you come in, because they'll need your cooperation. If your company consciously chooses to avoid the hassle of firing you, it can get you to quit, leave, get sick, or die. The company sets up the circumstances for your entrapment. Yet, none of these actual events are the company's responsibility.

I am not proposing that every company that wishes to let its employees go does so by intentional subterfuge. On the other hand, people who make the decisions to fire someone are no different from you and me. If there is a less painful way for them, it will be taken. Sometimes the path of least resistance is clearly marked by a company's careful plotting to pressure an individual out. We all have an inclination to believe this is what happened to us. While we are down and out, it makes us feel important to believe we were trapped or schemed against. Basic to the tension between you and your organization is the difference between your needs and demands and your company's needs and demands. This basic tension is magnified thousands of times by the secretiveness employed by those setting a Termination Trap.

There is your boss, either consciously plotting to get you out (and not be held accountable for it), or so uncomfortable about wanting you out that all he, or she, can do is behave in harmful ways (trying to cover his or her tracks). It is possible to feel under attack by a person who seems to be trying to do the right thing by getting you to leave on your own (in this case the "right thing" is for the company's benefit). Certainly it doesn't feel right to you, and this is just the beginning of the confusion. You don't know what all the indirect, murky signals mean, so it is difficult to understand what is happening. You tend to only react, with the reflex of a trapped animal. The inclination though, is to keep reacting for too long. Reacting can pose an insurmountable amount of trouble. If you react only to this immediate undefined threat, then you are at the mercy of your boss.

ACT, DON'T REACT

Figuring out what is really happening—why the job is going sour —gives you the ability to think, make plans, and test the plans out. If these plans don't work, you can think some more and devise new plans.

INSTEAD OF REACTING, YOU ARE INTERACTING.

This is the first step in taking back control of your job.

I place more value on understanding what is happening than feeling sorry or unhappy about it, and I hope you will, too. Having a job turn sour or getting fired can happen to anyone. There are many times when it is possible and desirable to save a job, and you can learn here how to do this. But, if getting fired is going to happen no matter what you do, or has already happened, then coping by putting the firing ordeal in perspective and gaining momentum to move beyond the quagmire of recrimination is the best way to go.

2

A PERSONAL CHECKLIST

IS THERE A TRAP LURKING IN YOUR FUTURE?

To understand just how the Termination Trap is set by you and your employer, you should first develop some very specific skills to help you correctly read the early warning signals. One place to begin looking for clues is in your personal life. It is not possible to determine from any single event in your personal life whether or not there are actually problems at work. However, some events are significant enough that it pays to think of them as potential clues.

The early warning signals of problems at work are often so subtle they are mistaken for nonwork-related tensions. It is important to recognize early uncomfortable feelings and appropriately attach them to the workplace. Too often we try to hide from the knowledge that the institution has begun to send indirect and direct signals that a trap has been set. After all, who wants to admit his or her job is in jeopardy. If you aren't careful you may attribute feelings of uneasiness about a job to something more acceptable like feeling sick because of the flu, or worry over an uncooperative child or spouse. This response is self-defeating on many levels. Remember to read all the signals; the trap takes different forms.

Do you find yourself not looking forward to going to work in the morning? Have you noticed that on Sunday afternoons and evenings you feel tired, queasy, or even physically ill? How many times in the recent past have you found yourself complaining to someone else about your job?

Sounds like a case of acute or chronic Sunday-itis. It is distinct from the better known Monday Morning Blues and far more insidious. If the Sunday symptoms were to occur on Friday evenings or Saturday mornings, then you might fairly conclude there were serious problems located somewhere in your personal life. Sunday symptoms might possibly signal that weekends are so wonderful nothing can compare to them. No problem here, except to figure out how to retire.

Unfortunately, usually Sunday symptoms herald the existence of problems on Monday, and the four days thereafter.

Coping with this situation means using it as a springboard to self-discovery. The following questions should lead you to a clear understanding of whether you are experiencing work-related difficulties. The only thing that might get in the way is being dishonest with yourself. So be very careful to never show your responses to these questions to anyone. Hopefully, this will give you the freedom to be totally honest with yourself. Now get a paper and pencil and write your responses down; saying the responses to yourself won't work, so be sure to *write* complete, honest responses. This isn't a quiz; there are no right or wrong answers.

1. Do you look forward to going to work after a weekend or vacation? Do you feel tired, queasy, or ill Sunday afternoons or evenings?

■ Force yourself to write down one thing about work which you do not look forward to. You must be very detailed; for example, "I can't stand my office, it's too dusty and dark," or "There are too many things to do and no one appreciates my work when I do it." Now comes the hard part.

■ Take the single item you don't like and list five distinct reasons why it is so unpleasant for you. Do not be terribly surprised if you find this embarassing. Reasons might be: "My parents always complimented me, but my boss doesn't," or "There aren't enough company parties and incentive programs," or "My boss likes Joe X. better than me."

2. Do you like the things you do in your job? Consider just the past six months in your job as you answer the next group of questions.

■ List five things you did in your job that you enjoyed and you are certain benefited the company.

■ Now, being very careful to be honest with yourself, list five things you did at work that you are certain were harmful to your job standing and/or to the company. Put down things you have done at work that were wrong or inadequate. Also write down any flaws in the fit between your personality and the demands of the job. This might be, "The job demands flexibility, and I tend to be methodical and somewhat rigid." This is a tough section for anyone to be honest about.

■ List five work-related circumstances which you know were not in your best personal interest and occurred because of the way the company is managed (or happened because of the nature of the task). It might be that you are a social worker dealing with violent clients, or maybe you are a used car salesman who has to work twelve hours a day, six days a week. It's possible that your boss is a tantrum thrower, or that your job calls for frequent three-martini lunches, and now you have a drinking problem.

■ List five things you, or others, have tried to accomplish at work, using the proper channels, that just somehow were never accepted by the company. Include a comment on how you feel about each of these situations.

■ Write at least one clear reason why the company cannot change the way you want it to.

3. List five things that your boss or people at work have suggested or implied that you should improve on.

■ Now, of those five, which ones did you not change even though you could have.

■ Which did you not change because you were absolutely certain you couldn't.

■ Now write down the exact reasons why you didn't or couldn't change. Be prepared to be tough with yourself here like, "I am not capable of doing this because I am not smart enough," or "I didn't do it because I resented the way he told me to do the job."

4. List the five ways you have been getting along better and/or worse in your personal life since you started this job. For example: Have you been drinking more? Did you make a close friend at work? Have you been more irritable? Has your job made you more sensitive to others' needs? Did you start (or stop) a regular program of exercise in conjuction with this job? Consider feelings as well as behaviors that are better or worse.

■ Next to each item, force yourself to make a connection between work and your personal life by writing down just how your job influenced those things which are better or worse.

5. Have you ever considered quitting your job? Do you daydream about doing other kinds of work, or the same work for another company? Do you know anyone who enjoys their work more than you do?

■ Before you took this job there must have been some things about it that gave you the feeling it would be a success. List at least five.

■ Now check the ones that have actually occurred.

■ List the successes that occurred though you thought they never would.

6. Would you leave your job to work for another company doing the same thing, if it could be done without major expenses, bitterness and strife, and inconvenience?

■ List five things that keep you in your job.

■ List five sacrifices you would be willing to make to change to a more enjoyable work situation.

WHAT TO DO
WITH YOUR LIST

Study this list for clues that a trap may be hiding in your job which makes you feel uncomfortable just at the end of the weekend. Use the list to determine how much you like work and how much "it" doesn't like you. If the list reveals problems at work, make an immediate appointment with your boss and do the following:

■ Do not reveal the list, but bring in notes that will help direct your meeting. The idea is to sleuth out the sources of your discomfort.

■ Ask for an appraisal of your work.

■ If your boss fails to mention your strongest points bring them up, and notice if your boss glosses over them, or seems aware and impressed by them.

■ Then ask why he or she did not bring up your weak points or failures (the ones you were so honest about in the list above). Be careful to do this in a positive context; for example, "I've been thinking a lot lately about some of your criticisms and I've begun working on them. I am wondering how my progress has been sitting with you."

Listen with a third ear to any clues to the existence of more active problems. Take notes in front of your boss.

Your list can be revealing to you in other ways. Just being honest in this self-appraisal should feel good to you. But, your responses should help you see just how much reinforcement you need to feel good about work. There will be clues about your private, preconceived notions about how work should be, and how these notions may have created trouble and a lack of pleasure for you at work. You can begin to get a sense of how powerful personal expectations and needs that were unrelated to work got transferred (unfairly, and maybe unexpectedly) to job issues. I hope that the insights will help you evaluate how much of the problem is the job and how much is within yourself. You'll begin to see if you are setting your own trap, or if it is being set for you. As painful as this process is, you will then be able to identify areas where there are reasonable expectations for change.

ALCOHOL AND DRUG USE

Do you drink more than fifteen beers throughout an entire week, or more than three beers on any given day? Do you have two hard liquor, or mixed, drinks almost every day? Is your shot bigger than the standard 30cc jigger? Do you drink three martinis a day? Do you drink the same number of hard liquor drinks, but lately you've been pouring more into the shot glass? Have you started using marijuana? Have you begun using Valium or Librium on your doctor's advice? Have you been using cocaine, or stronger drugs? Did you just read these questions and answer them dishonestly?

No matter what your friends are doing, no matter what some doctor has told you, *if you answered yes to any of the above questions you are on the way to a potentially serious problem.* Read the previous sentence one more time. Remember that some doctors, too, are serious abusers of all kinds of drugs, so it isn't always safe to check it out with a physician.

Changes in drug and alcohol use signal problems that are often work-related. It is always worthwhile to retrace your steps, looking for correlations between changes in alcohol and drug use in conjunction with changes in your personal life. This bit of careful sleuthing is a search for "proximal cause": the nearest event in time to the beginning or increase in use of alcohol and drugs. Consider also what might be contributing factors: loneliness on sales trips, difficulty belonging to the work group, tension and anxiety acquired during the course of work that sticks to you during your personal time, high performance pressure from inside of you or from goals established by management, or looking for relaxation in a bottle or a pill. Of course there can be personal issues contributing to drug overuse, and these issues are beyond the scope of this book. However, the use of alcohol and drugs is, at the very least, probably damaging to work performance. Here's what you should do if you even have the beginning of a drug problem.

■ Go for help right now. First approach a member of your family, someone with insight and/or a prior history of overcoming a personal problem. You are looking for understanding, not reassurance or denial. You want to talk with a person who will accept that there is a drug problem for you, and not try to pretend that nothing is wrong.

■ The next step is to go to a private, noncompany physician of your choosing and state that you have a problem. Be careful to not ask if you have a problem. Many physicians have as much trouble seeing alcohol and drug abuse as a problem as anyone else in our society does. Ask for specific treatment resources in your community. If alcohol is your problem, then consider going to AA; their success rate is far greater than the medical profession's.

■ Be very cautious about two things when you talk with your doctor. First, it is a doctor's inclination to treat one form of drug abuse by prescribing another abusable drug (i.e., Librium, Xanax, or Valium). Second, there is the possibility that your physician may not be prepared to handle a drug abuse problem. The best thing to do is ask for, even demand, referral for evaluation and treatment.

■ If your doctor cannot be of help, consider calling your local community mental health center. This facility is not just for the poor or chronically mentally ill people. These centers are mandated to be of service to everyone, and you may be pleasantly surprised to discover how geared up and ready the staffs are to manage drug-related problems. One last ditch effort to consider is to approach whatever referral and/or treatment resources are available to you in your present workplace. There is one major risk here associated with confidentiality: just how much information makes it into your personnel file.

It does not matter if your job is the cause of the drug use. Drugs create their own personalities in the users. Drugs are a parachute that help you bail out in the present, and then leave you less competent to deal with the future. Drugs and alcohol are a short-term solution that renders the long-term more precarious. If your job is not the cause of the drug problem, then the drugs will cause a job problem sooner or later.

DIFFERENT STRESSES
CAN SIGNAL A TRAP

Throughout the remainder of the book there will be vignettes with analyses and particular coping suggestions. Rather than just listing a series of "do's" and "don't's" and expecting you to accept them on good faith, I have chosen to present events which actually happened to place the analyses and solutions in a clear context. You should be able to relate parts of each and every vignette to specific circumstances that exist in your work experience. None of the examples given in the book are unusual or unique. The solutions presented can be used in many of your work situations to prevent, as well as solve, getting trapped.

The first vignettes illustrate just how physical and emotional signals of being trapped at work can present themselves in your personal life.

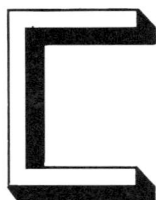

THE
SPLEEN
MACHINE

Jim was impossible during the week. It had gotten to the point where both kids asked if they could eat dinner early, in order to avoid his unrelenting sarcasm at the dinner table. If it wasn't something on the news, then it was traffic, the food, or someone's table manners. Weekends were different, then he wasn't so irritable. But somehow, nothing could make up for the punishment he meted out with his new-found acidity. There was no calming the beast in him. Any attempt to be understanding and compassionate with him seemed to escalate his slicing comments.

Ellen finally had it and told him so, right in front of the kids. Yelling and screaming, the tears pouring down her face, she cut loose with four weeks of pent-up frustration.

Jim seemed barely fazed by her unusual outburst. Instead he sliced his way closer to her weak points with one sarcastic statement after another. It was his son who brought everything to a halt when he asked, "Dad, just who are you fighting? We're supposed to be on your side."

There was a second of paralyzed silence; then Jim broke into tears. Ellen reached for him as he sobbed. For two hours the four of them sat together, no one understanding what was happening beyond sensing a reduction in the tension.

Later, in family therapy, Ellen voiced how afraid she had been that Jim was having a nervous breakdown. Jim responded with his old sarcasm. "With a boss like mine, who wouldn't."

This was the first clear indication to Jim, as well as to his family, that there were problems at work. From then on, Jim slowly searched, with his family's help, for the sources of all of his stress. The only clue to work problems had been Jim's sarcasm put onto the rest of the family.

ANALYSIS

THE PAIN OF BEING TRAPPED AT WORK
IS OFTEN SCREAMED OUT AT HOME

You may be one of those people who never discusses work with your spouse or friends. The point here is that the "you" at work is the "you" at home; the same person with the same feelings and thoughts. There may be a firm boundary in your mind between work and your personal life, but your feelings remain inside you. If your feelings about work are negative then they sit inside you, pent-up, waiting to be unleashed. Students of human behavior have known for a long time that human excrement flows downhill. A person who is maltreated in one situation may unconsciously pass it on to someone else. There is a song that suggests "(We) only hurt the ones (we) love," and the Spleen Machine verifies that. It takes a lot of love and trust to stay with someone whose personality takes a mean turn.

COPING

USING YOUR CARING RELATIONSHIPS
AS AN EARLY WARNING SYSTEM

The displacement of feelings acquired at work onto the family doesn't have to get as far as it did in this example. It is always important to use your caring and loving relationships as an early warning signal for problems at work.

■ Consider asking your family and friends to let you know if they ever feel that you are getting too tense or irritable.

■ Work on developing skills to separate the content of your criticisms from the tone that you use to convey the criticisms. You don't want to put the people you love on the back of their heels in their relationships with you. Nothing could be worse than having your major support system feel chronically defensive when you are around.

■ Remember that your boss can be a Spleen Machine and dump all sorts of negative feelings onto you. You will need to know enough about your boss's personality to know when this is happening. You also need enough confidence in yourself to not take these attacks personally—easier said then done.

■ In the same way you need the people who love you to be on your side and be generally supportive, they have needs, too. There is that dangerous dinner time when families reconstitute themselves after each person has suffered a day's worth of trials and tribulations. Along with the food, there is served up damaged egos, elation, and frustrations. If you are a parent, you may experience a strong need to maintain that magical stereotype of being the always loving, invincible parent who can handle anything. If this is the case, then you may have some difficulty in airing your problems and continue to pent up your feelings. Inevitably, one day you will inadvertently release those feelings on unsuspecting loved ones. The best antidote for this is the daily, regular presenting of the vulnerable, uncertain sides of yourself to everyone who loves you. They, as well as you, need to be reminded that it's only at work where we are expected to be always strong and invincible, perfectly in control and well composed.

THE TELLTALE HEART

STRESS CAUSES
PHYSICAL SYMPTOMS

You are lying in bed and you hear, "Lub-dub, lub-dub, lub-dub." It's your heart beating, right there in your ear. Every night when you try to go to sleep it sits in your ear, too loud to be reassuring. More often then not it keeps you awake (or something does). Your appetite can go. At first it isn't too noticeable because you were a little out of shape to begin with. Then your energy drifts away, slowly and imperceptibly. You might feel tired a lot of the time. Maybe your concentration has slipped, but you won't think of it that way. Most people who have trouble concentrating blame it on their memory. Then they remember how often they have trouble with their memory, so that can't be much of a problem. Sometimes people notice they are having more frequent colds or sinus infections. For others it is headaches, or flu symptoms, muscle aches, or indigestion. Most usual with The Telltale Heart is a diminished sense of pleasure, as if it were being drowned out.

Bodily symptoms are so powerful that they often become the focal point for the worrying, and the actual source of the stress remains hidden. Of course, there can be many sources of dread in one's life, not just work. But work problems alone can produce that awful, tense feeling that something is about to happen that isn't very pleasant. Too many physicians treat just the symptoms and signs of stress without searching for the source.

If you are experiencing these physical symptoms, consult a good doctor for a physical exam. It is important to be certain just why your body is sending you these signals. If you have a battle on your hands to save your job, then it is worthwhile to find out you are healthy. Your physician will be able to determine how fit you are to enter into the problems at work more directly. It also is probably true that it has been a long time since you had a thorough physical exam. Usually, but not always, people with recent physical exams gain a sense of reassurance and well-being from knowing there is nothing wrong with their bodies. But, a good physical exam will not remove the stress from your job.

Take your spouse, significant other,or roommate with you to the doctor's. Whoever lives with you is probably already aware that something is wrong, and they deserve to be a part of the checkup. This also serves to establish who your allies are just at the time when you are awakening to the sources of the stress in your life.

TIME WARP

THE LOSS OF ENJOYMENT
AND PLEASURE
IS A PAINFUL CLUE

Slowly but surely you run out of time to do the things which had always been important to you. Maybe it was skiing, or running, or woodworking, hiking, stamp collecting, gardening, or just plain old puttering around. Could be anything particularly pleasurable. What happens is there is no time to do it anymore.

What has been lost is the energy, joy, hope, or strength—not time. Sapped by some problem, maybe one at work, you are unable to keep your head above water any longer to do the things that are life-savers (or givers). Something has dragged you under and robbed you of the ability to enjoy yourself.

There is probably nothing more important than having some time to oneself. For some people it's like recharging depleted batteries, for other people it's filling one's cup to brim. This isn't just time with family and friends, it's time to be alone and pursue one's own interests. Free time is freedom from other people's needs. Free time is time for loving and caring for oneself. Free time is giving enough to oneself to be sure there is enough to go around for everyone else.

If you have lost your enjoyment of life, run for help. Try not to be afraid to feel depressed. Allowing yourself to feel natural reactions is far more healthy for you than creating additional stresses by trying to suppress the feelings. Depression is not an illness in many cases; it can be a natural symptom and sign of stress.

Search for the source of the Time Warp. It is very important to ask why you've lost time. Are you running scared at work? Are they using you, and are you allowing them to do that?

If work is the source of the Time Warp then consider an honest appraisal of how long you can last without replenishing yourself. It is also worthwhile to look clearly at your motives for depleting yourself. Is there any chance that your work demands to be first on your list of importance, even before your own survival? Are you willing to draw a boundary between your personal and professional lives which gives you enough room to enjoy what it is you are working so hard for?

Spend some time right now examining some of your principles which may be getting you into trouble. Also spend some time looking at the personal demands placed upon you by your job.

THE
HELPFUL
HARPY

By now Bart did not want to go home anymore. He'd no sooner walk in the door when Evelyn would ask him how work had gone. It wasn't the question as much as the melted, worried look on her face. Then at dinner she'd ask him again to tell her about the problems he was having at work. The only problem Bart felt he had was his wife's worry that something was wrong at work. She was insufferable with all of her questions.

When confronted, she agreed that she was very worried for his job. Hearing this he promptly attacked her for worrying about the money. She tried to convince him that it wasn't the money, she just felt he was under a lot of pressure and she worried about him. This response reminded him too much of his mother's concern. When he was younger, his mother always worried about things that never seemed to bother him. So it wasn't long before he was yelling at Evelyn for treating him like a little boy. The harder she tried to get him to talk about work, the angrier he became.

After almost six months of her worrying he came home to tell her the company had fired him. Then he poured out to her how rough work had been for over a year.

ANALYSIS
FEELINGS ARE CONTAGIOUS

In Bart's case he was infected with a ton of corporate ill-will without being aware of it. For Bart it was just too painful to think about while it was happening. This is called denial, or repression of painful, unacceptable feelings. For someone sensitive enough, there are tiny little signals that can be read. This is what Evelyn did. When Bart became angry with her he displaced his feelings from a painful, unacceptable area of his work-life onto a more obvious, receptive problem (Evelyn's "helpful harping"). Bart totally missed the truth because it was too painful.

COPING

BY REMEMBERING

THIS CAN HAPPEN

The best thing to do is try and remember this example. Denial is often so strong that nothing as intellectual as a suggestion from me will make a difference. However, knowing that the problem exists may allow you to see that a Helpful Harpy is really a Caring Spouse.

The point of this chapter has been to help you look at your own personal life as a valuable tool for measuring and managing work-related stress. It is not unusual for the earliest of all clues of a job going sour to present themselves as stresses outside of work. Remember, we carry home from work what was handed to us; if we are not careful, we give this over to the people we love. Then they react to our work stresses, sometimes even fight them off.

USE CONFLICT AND TENSION AT HOME
AS A POTENTIAL INDICATOR OF
WORK-RELATED STRESS.

If you do, there is great opportunity for staying on top of your work problems.

3

HOW
ORGANIZATIONS
WORK:
ARE TRAPS
PART OF
THE STRUCTURE?

C onnecting physical and behavioral symptoms of stress with feeling trapped at work is an important first step. How to locate the source of work stress is the next step. We are inclined to narrow our focus in the hurried search for the source of any discomfort. Personality traits are more easily identifiable than abstract concepts such as how people communicate, lines of authority, decision-making matrices, and information gathering patterns. The clash of personalities seems to be the obvious source for all stress, but often this is not the case. In fact, some pressures at work are simply a result of how the company is organized. Let us look at how company organization can influence the way you experience stress, and the ensuing feelings of entrapment.

Organizations can be divided into four major categories. Looking at the table, you should be able to locate the company you work with. A company that is organized around habitual behaviors has to manage people who perform repetitive, stereotypical actions to manufacture a product. This company will be different from a problem-solving company which needs to manage to enhance the employees' abilities to create designs. The first company has boredom to contend with; the second, anarchy and eccentricity. This leads to the first points about organizations.

TYPES OF ORGANIZATIONS*

TYPE OF ORGANIZATION	MAJOR FUNCTION	EXAMPLES	EFFECTIVENESS CRITERION
Habit	Replicating standard and uniform products	Highly mechanized factories, etc.	Number of products
Problem-solving	Creating new ideas	Research groups; engineering divisions, organizations, etc.	Number of design ideas
Indoctrination	Changing habits, attitudes, intellect, behavior (both physical and mental)	Universities, prisons, hospitals, etc.	Number of clients leaving
Service	Distributing services either directly to consumer, or to above types	Military, govt. advertising, taxi companies, etc.	Extent of services performed

*This chart is taken directly from Bennis, WG "Leadership Theory and Administrative Behavior: The Problem of Authority," Administrative Science Quarterly, Vol. 4, #3, p. 299, December, 1959.

■ The type of organization and its task determines management style.

■ A company can be designed with many different, often conflicting, goals.

■ In any organization the needs of the company often conflict with the needs of the employees.

■ The needs of people as individuals are very often different from those same people when they belong to groups.

Let's take a look at how these points can create stress. Remember, none of this has to do with the personalities of particular individuals. For example, an upper level management team could decide to run its company in a way to maximize short-term gains at the expense of long-term growth and profit. In a service industry, maximizing short-term profits can lead to an administrative decision to limit vacation time, double each individual's work load, and promote overtime work by limiting salary increases for those people refusing to do the extra work.

In a service industry, the major impact of management decisions falls upon employees (the product is a service provided by the employees). Employees feel increased tension at work and in their personal lives because the short-term profits are produced directly from their increased output of services. There is an acceleration of communications to the point where time for feedback and clarification is severely limited. Resources become increasingly limited, and there is an increase in intra-company competitiveness. All this happens as a direct result of a management decision linked to the function and organization of a company.

MAXIMIZING SHORT-TERM
PROFITS HINDERS HUMANISM

Short-term profit is a recent highly valued goal for many corporations. Work stresses and job jeopardies increase when an organization maximizes the bottom line. The major task confronting organizations is their ability to respond to changing conditions. The immediate goal is product profitability, and a distant second (if at all) is concern about the employee stress that often accompanies the short-term profit objective. The humanistic areas of corporate concern are often the first to be devalued in a rapidly reacting competitive system. The end result is that all employees are increasingly vulnerable to personal attrition. It leaves each employee alone in the struggle to manage stress at work.

ORGANIZATIONS HAVE DIFFERENT PARTS. EACH PART CAN CONFLICT WITH THE OTHERS.

Not only is there a conflict between company needs and individual employee needs (which is often exacerbated by stressful short-term goals), but there also is conflict between intracompany divisions as they vie for limited corporate resources. Heaped on top of all these dynamics is the often unspoken but well-known need to accommodate top level management. How all of this impacts on unsuspecting employees can be seen in the next few examples.

TROJAN HORSE
SEDUCTION AS A WAY
TO OBTAIN
PERSONAL SACRIFICES

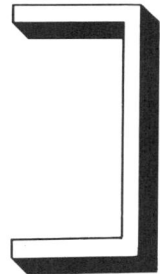

John was a successful, well-liked, third-level manager who enjoyed his job in a national company. One day his boss called him in and suggested that he take an important promotion. It was out of the blue. On the surface the promotion seemed terrific: new title, more pay, and he didn't have to relocate. The job was two floors up. John's head and heart were saying "yes," but a tight knot in his stomach said "no." While standing there he remembered that two highly regarded, third-level managers had been in that position within the last four years. He wasn't sure if he had forgotten, or maybe he was never told, where they were now. So, he asked. His boss responded with a barrage of compliments about John's abilities, the reasons the company needed him, and why John couldn't say no.

By now the hard sell was obvious, and that awareness made it easier for John to politely defer until he could think it through. Within the next few days he was able to piece together a picture of his new job. The division he was to head had too many "dead-wood" employees, too much risky product, and it was the pet project of the president of the company.

John declined the promotion after a careful discussion with his wife. His manager was initially furious with him. John had anticipated this pressure, as well as the pressure his boss must have been under to find someone for the slot. He offered up two of his own (unwanted) employees for the promotion. It worked. John was careful to follow the course of the person who took the job. Two years later, she was quickly fired from the company for poor performance. It seemed clear to John that the division existed only to please the president. Without the president's support the division would have been folded long ago; but he was so invested in the project that he couldn't see its futility, and the undermining lack of support through various levels of management. Rather, the president held the person running it accountable for its failure.

ANALYSIS

TAKING SOME JOBS IS EQUIVALENT
TO COMMITTING PROFESSIONAL SUICIDE

Futile jobs are sometimes created to control destructive feelings between different parts of companies. The scapegoat who takes the futile job helps relieve tensions between different parts of a company.

There is always the possibility that a company is trying to find a way to get rid of someone without the employee's knowledge. In John's case, this was not true, because who got pushed out was irrelevant as long as someone was offered up as a sacrifice to the president's pet project. Rather than upper level management confronting the president with the problems associated with the pet project and resolving the tension between the task of the company and the personal agenda of the president, something else happened. Employees were being promoted into a no-win position.

The issue in Trojan Horse is that management needed to find someone to do a futile job. There really was no attempt to balance the personal needs of the individual employee and his or her career against the corporate needs for survival. This scenario is most obviously played out in the military, where human lives are routinely offered up to get a task accomplished. The military is conscious that it asks for the supreme sacrifice and struggles administratively to cushion the reality of the request. Many companies also consider their employees to be consumable. Work is so stressful, some tasks are so impossible, that the bad jobs are sweetened with high financial rewards, promotions, and good benefits.

If John had accepted the promotion, he would have stepped into a trap that would have ended with his termination. There was nothing personal about the situation. It arose because of a certain organizational structure within John's company.

COPING
MEANS AVOIDING
THE SEDUCTION TRAP

■ Examine John's handling of Trojan Horse as a model for successfully handling this problem.

■ Hold off on the decision to accept any new position long enough to study the proposition. A change like this is comparable to taking an entirely new job, so asking for the time to think is a legitimate request.

■ Separate the pleasure of getting the offer from the reality of the task to be done. Avoid being seduced.

■ Be prepared to suffer your boss's annoyance when you turn a promotion down. Remember there are pressures on your boss that forced him or her to offer you a Trojan Horse to begin with. It is remotely possible that your boss is (was) simply an isolated rotten egg, but you should have known that before the offer anyway.

■ Double-check with your boss about the possibility that he or she wanted you to go because you were not doing adequate enough work, or maybe you were causing problems. Wait a while before doing this. You don't want to hurt the feelings of someone who gave you what they considered to be a valid offer.

MANAGEMENT CAN
BE A SOURCE OF STRESS

All activities in a company have to be regulated, much in the same way that our bodies are carefully monitored and regulated by physiologic mechanisms. What the regulator in a company (from now on called a manager) does is monitor the different company functions and control the flow of resources between two, or more, discontinuous parts.

Managers have to regulate by shifting limited resources among employees with oftentimes conflicting activities. This is the major source of stress for a manager and accounts for the unloading of impossible goals onto unknowing workers. For example, in a taxicab company, there is often the need to spend limited capital on new radios, and to recruit new cab drivers, and to purchase new cabs and licenses—all happening at once. But rarely are the goals met all at once, especially if an increase in gasoline costs gobbles up some anticipated profits. It is the manager who must set priorities, taking many variables into account (including, hopefully, the needs of the human beings in the company).

Many managers try to avoid conflicts by keeping their employees ignorant of the issue of limited resources. The following is an example.

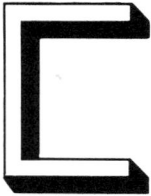

FOREIGN AID
THANK YOU
FOR NOTHING

You make a request for the allocation of specific supplies or services to get your job done. Your boss, or the company, responds with verbal support. When the supplies or services arrive they are not quite what you asked for, or they may even be totally irrelevant to your work. Things slow down, and it's hard for you to struggle through and get the job done. Much time is spent sending back what you didn't ask for or need, and convincing someone to give you what you asked for.

Capping this off, your boss walks in one day and is visibly upset. He has supported your work, authorized the expensive Foreign Aid and now your task isn't finished on time.

ANALYSIS
WITHHOLDING OBJECTS IS A WAY TO CONTROL OTHERS
AND TAKE THE PRESSURE OFF THE MANAGER

In spite of the irrelevance of the company's response to your request, be certain to be grateful and show it. You have been kept in the dark, so it isn't quite clear why the resources that were promised you (for some job that your boss has convinced you is terribly important) weren't forthcoming. What confines your frustration is the fact that the institution did respond to your request. When people give something they like to be appreciated. With real foreign aid, the recipient country is supposed to show a public display of gratitude. No matter that CARE packages were filled with powdered milk and over 75 percent of the world's non-Caucasian adult population can't digest the sugar in cow's milk. No matter that the powdered milk products get fed to livestock rather than humans. What mattered was that the receiving countries expressed gratitude.

There is the chance that you are dealing with a human error here. These are bound to happen by chance in about 3 percent of all human actions. Sombody may have tried very hard to do a good job for the company and you. Wouldn't you want credit for an honest effort?

It is quite probable that you were assigned a task that your boss did feel was important. Somehow you weren't told that other tasks shared equal priority in a situation where there were limited resources. Instead of making the tough decision to not support your task, your boss leaves you with the tail end of the limited resources.

COPING
WITH COMPANY SUPPORT
THAT IS USELESS

■ Acknowledge the support while clarifying the original request.

■ Use copies of requests, memos, and minutes of meetings to document the task support.

■ Attempt to clarify the nature of the other tasks that are competing for the resources you didn't get. See if you can find out just how it was that promises for allocations were made without the company being able to follow through.

■ Avoid emotional displays and bad-mouthing your suppliers. Remember they have pressures on them also. Get the data first, then find a safe place (family, friends, an objective boss) to sort through the problem.

THE MANAGER'S DILEMMA: CONFLICTING ALLEGIANCES TO DIFFERENT GROUPS' NEEDS

This is an important source of impersonal stress in all companies. What one manager needs to get the job done often conflicts with some other manager's needs. Immense tension which filters through to all employees is created in trying to resolve these conflicts. None of this tension is caused by personalities; rather it comes from the reality of finite resources and the problem of their allocation.

Let's use a small hypothetical company as an example. Some crucial administrative decisions can be made by all lower administrative level employees. In a taxi company, each driver must decide the quickest, most economical route between the pick-up and drop-off points. Without expertise at this level, a cab company couldn't survive. But those same cab drivers cannot decide which of thirty different phone calls to the central office should be responded to. If drivers did make that decision, they might be inclined to pick up only those fares nearest them. What is in one driver's best interests (nearest, quickest, and most lucrative fares) may not be beneficial to the company at all times. This is one clear example of a conflict between the needs of the individual and the needs of the corporation. Many companies have procedures or rules for dealing with these divergent needs to avoid conflict and dissension.

The decisions to send taxis to different points are often made by a first-level manager, a dispatcher, who has a broad view of where all the cabs are and what routes are most economic. This person uses a radio to send and receive information and is paid (in our make-believe company) a certain percentage of the company's profits as an incentive for making decisions that are in the company's best interest.

The cab drivers are somewhat suspect of the dispatcher's motives; when sending a driver to a particular place to pick up a fare, is the dispatcher interested in helping the drivers or the company? The larger question is: don't managers have to be able to balance the needs of the company with the needs of its employees? And don't they need the support of top level management to do this?

As an employee, then, it is extremely helpful to step back from the day-to-day interpersonal activities of your workplace, and acknowledge the sources of stress that are clearly a function of the nature of the task, the profit goals, and the availability of resources.

You may be surprised at how therapeutic this new perspective can be, and how revitalized you'll feel by the simple realization that your stress is not a personal problem between you and your manager.

There are two sources of stress that do involve personalities as they relate to the structure and function of organizations. One is that certain character traits in management can exaggerate stressful feelings; the other is that the nature of group behavior in the workplace can be a source of stress. You'll find it is more difficult to distance yourself from these forces because they feel so personal, so increasing your awareness of the cause of these tensions will be a big help.

SOME CHARACTER TRAITS
THAT INFLUENCE STRESS

Individuals have an internal life of feelings, beliefs, and thoughts, all constructed into experience, knowledge, and skills. Decisions impact on people's feelings as well as their behaviors. Managers who are sensitive to their own feelings and have empathy for others are able to artfully blend the needs of the company and the needs of its employees. There is no doubt that a manager's personality traits can have a profound impact on your job. Take the following, for example . . .

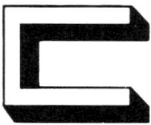

SHMOE

This is the boss who is genuinely afraid of hurting anybody. So what this person does is unknowingly hurt most everybody. This person believes that it is horrible to be direct and forthright, thinking that other people can't handle it. Sometimes Shmoes understand that they are the people who can't handle being direct. No matter, the devastation is the same, with or without the insight.

Instead of firing someone, a Shmoe might say, "Are you sure you wouldn't be happier working somewhere else?" When something goes wrong there is a look of sadness or hurt, and a verbal denial that anything is wrong. People don't get fired by Shmoes. They are reassigned, or they just quit for personal reasons.

The Shmoe is a master of understatement. Employees are left with the responsibility for interpreting every look, every change in voice intonation, each memo, and every decision as potential traps for being terminated. People who work for Shmoes get fired thousands of times just worrying about it. They suffer from hypertension and anxiety attacks, and they have little respect for the Shmoes that make them so unhappy. There is a pervasive threatening environment at work.

Shmoes are genuinely afraid of almost everything interpersonal. With their authority and power, they end up infecting everybody with their fears. Their belief that not being direct is the kindest way to handle others is devastating when acted upon. Their weakness in the complexities of human interaction renders them rigid stereotypes of goodness and humanitarianism. God is always on the side of someone who tries really hard to not hurt a fellow human being, say the Shmoes of the world. Their beliefs are struck in stone, while the wet cement of their oblique communications goes creeping up your ankles.

Shmoes are also unable to handle aggression directed toward them. Being in control at all times takes precedence over everything. They can be so tense about losing control of their own aggressive feelings that they have no understanding or compassion for the pain their behavior inflicts on others. Their wish to hurt no one sets a large Termination Trap. You've never felt the risk of getting caught in that trap so acutely until you've worked for one of these humanitarians.

Companies put Shmoes into positions of authority as conduits of power for the non-Shmoes above. Despite their ineptness, Shmoes serve a valuable function in certain organizations: they enable people above or below them to control the nature and character of the work. The true Shmoe is a patsy for others who exert power over the workplace.

Don't waste time trying to change this person. Most of all, do not try to show them how damaging their behavior is. These people have too many social and religious forces to hide behind. Keep in constant awareness that you are supposed to sense traps lurking about all the time.

You'll just have to develop your own criteria for adequate job performance without monitoring your boss's indirect signals all the time. It is too upsetting, too stressful.

Never wait for a Shmoe to be fired. There is no place for this person to hide, everybody knows his or her problem. If you go to upper levels of management to discuss (tell on) a Shmoe, do not expect management to be surprised (though they may act it). You will only establish yourself as a tattler. You must assume that Shmoes rise to the levels they did because the company has use for them there.

The turmoil from a Shmoe can last forever, so do not automatically ride out the storm as a coping mechanism. First decide how much stamina you have, and just how much pain and tension your personal life can endure.

HUMBLE PIE

Peter had worked his way up to chief dispatcher at a transportation company within three years. He had been the chief for the past six months. It was a high pressure job, lots of scheduling and delivery problems, not the least of which was managing five other dispatchers. He never noticed any connection between his job and two duodenal ulcer bleeds, constant headaches, and frequent weekend alcohol binges. Three hospitalizations and multiple trips to his doctor for migraines were a lot for somebody just turned twenty-nine.

HUMBLE PIE
All you can eat
10¢

Eventually his internist referred him to a psychiatrist. Peter had no idea what was bothering him. His personal life, friendships, finances, and creativity seemed very much in order. His job was stressful, but the people interested him. There were also the excellent pay and benefits.

The first clue to the problem surfaced during psychotherapy. Peter was feeling guilty at work. No matter how pleased he was with his work, there was always the feeling that he could have done more. He felt that no matter what he did the compliments never came. His psychiatrist had to help him sort out whether or not they actually did appreciate him at work.

A typical transaction with his boss was "Nice job, Peter, but . . ." Then would follow very pointed criticisms of how he could have done better. Peter would find himself repeatedly apologizing to his boss, in spite of the fact that just before the criticism he had felt confident with his work performance.

Peter went ahead with brief therapy to hunt for the sources of his guilt. He realized that this guilt was a hidden anger toward his boss turned inward against himself. He saw how this connected to his earlier fears of being angry with his father for some unfair recognition he had gotten as a child. The new insights led to changes in his behaviors and feelings at work. First he stopped the drinking, then the tension and guilt abated. It took him four years of freedom from medical problems to regain confidence in his ability to cope at work. Peter kept his job, and continued to do well.

ANALYSIS
WITHHOLDING PRAISE IS
A WAY TO KEEP CONTROL

It may seem at first glance that the problem illustrated here is unique to Peter. We all bring unique combinations of experiences, predilections, needs, and expectations to work with us every day. All these affect how we react and interact on the job. You must be wary of a job where compliments are scarce and work is just there to be done. This kind of starvation renders a person more likely to hunger for resolving more personal, prior deprivations.

Humble Pie is rarely on the menu; bosses don't even realize they are serving it up to their employees. Almost invariably everybody is eating pieces of varying size. It is for this reason that one must understand what is happening and not just react to it. Humble Pie is something that is force fed in those companies where compliments are always followed by criticisms. Somehow nothing is ever enough. Humble Pie derives from some unspoken theory of discomfort at work. This is most likely a Calvinistic spin-off that work is not meant to be enjoyable. Therefore, if you pay your employees well, give them lots of responsibility and authority, as well as security, there has to be some way to make them feel uncomfortable. Anger toward the conveyor of the Pie usually evokes a bigger piece for you to choke on: "What's the matter? Don't you enjoy your job?" or, "Don't we pay you enough?" or, "Of course I appreciate your work; didn't you get a big raise last quarter?"

What makes Humble Pie so difficult to deal with is that the people who choke on it are the ones most performance-oriented and vulnerable to guilt. This mechanism is often most prevalent in those businesses free of union intervention because the employees are overly grateful (dependent) for all their employers have done.

COPING
WITH UNCERTAIN REWARDS AT WORK

■ Understand what your company's signals are for recognizing good job performance. Work is not necessarily a place to be loved. Doing a good job has to be recognized by pay, advancement, and increasing authority and responsibility first. If feeling good came first then there might be a problem of worker exploitation or severe employer paternalism.

■ When the compliment is followed by a "but" with ensuing criticism, listen carefully and say something like: "I understand that I did a good job, and I am always working to make things better. I did hear your criticisms and I will work on them." Do not be surprised if your boss then looks a little surprised. Bosses don't know when they are serving Humble Pie.

■ As always, keep your cool. Consider sharing these occurrences with your spouse, close friends outside of work, or a psychotherapist.

LITTLE BIG HORN

Sandra had just finished her MBA and was already a vice president at the bank. She was careful about speaking openly at weekly division meetings. Something made her feel uncomfortable. Soon she was losing sleep. Then the unbearable tension drove her into a psychiatrist's office. It didn't take long to uncover that Sandra was very afraid. After years of durable self-confidence this was a new feeling for her. Work was going well for her, she felt appreciated and well compensated. She did notice that her symptoms were worse on Sundays and then again Friday mornings before the division meetings.

Within three psychotherapy sessions Sandra began discussing how tense she felt in the Friday administrative meetings. Sandra felt that it was stimulating to challenge ideas at work. It seemed to her that the heat of conflict could bring out the best ideas. She had the expectation that her boss would watch the ideas evolve out of the conflict and then choose the one that seemed the best to him. Instead she noticed he would make comments to group members which seemed to set everybody fighting with one another. If two people disagreed, it often occurred over issues where there was no right or wrong. As each meeting went on there would come a logical time for resolution of disagreements, but resolution never came. Sandra did not like it, and she worried when her turn for conflict would come around.

Sandra realized what bothered her the most was what happened after her boss decided which side of the argument the bank would support. At that point of decision, her boss would turn to the person carrying the losing viewpoint and criticize that person for his, or her, "bad," "silly," "ridiculous," even "dumb" idea. Then members of the group would proceed to speak up openly against the person and the idea in an overly critical, aggressive manner. Sandra felt the tension in the room was palpable. Once she noticed tears in one attacked person's eyes. She connected these occurrences to the loss of her confidence. Sandra found herself in the difficult position of having ideas and wanting to present them for discussion, but she was afraid of the attack that might follow. She felt the entire group was a large reservoir of angry competition between the people. The ideas seemed almost secondary to getting even with someone for some past hurt or attack.

ANALYSIS
PERSONAL ATTACKS
DIFFUSE POWER

Again, the problem here flows from management style. If the boss openly encouraged aggressive discussion of the *issues* only, then Sandra, as well as others, would feel free to participate. The company would then benefit from the creative brainstorming sessions. No one would hold back because no one would be blamed or branded; the good ideas would rise to the surface.

However, in Little Big Horn, management presents the illusion of tolerating open disagreement to cover its tracks. This illusion is at the expense of individuals as well as good ideas. Some managers cannot feel confident with their own decisions without labeling the rejected idea makers and/or the ideas as all bad. Labeling some ideas good enables the managers to dilute the greater truth that decisions about new ideas are usually gray area compromises that have yet to be tested. It's a form of self-protection to have someone else come up with the questionable answer. It creates an illusion for the future in case the good idea turns sour. The illusion is that your boss had only one choice at the time the decision was made for the company. Because all other suggestions were inadequate and came from terrible sources, the boss ends up doing the only right thing. The existence of Little Big Horn in a company reveals a confusion between recognizing valid employee differences versus labeling those differences as marks of inferiority. This transaction almost invariably leads to hostile competitiveness between employees.

If you aren't careful, you may walk right into the Termination Trap by getting angry with your boss, the person who instigates the fight. Your boss will appear shocked, point to his or her excellent management style and record, and then promptly attack you personally for being so wrong.

This transaction resembles an even more personal one: Hedda Hopper. In this work-related problem, it is the personality of the idea producer that is judged and attacked, not the idea. This is a more lethal trap because it can be done so subtly. It is almost impossible to avoid angry outbursts and retaliations if you are the one attacked. If the attacked person riles up too far, the attacker can suddenly become a lamb by saying: "Well I don't understand what you are so upset about. All I was talking about was the idea you presented. You know, you shouldn't take things so personally." Suddenly you've been labeled "suspicious," even "paranoid," and those words were never uttered. At this stage things are almost completely out of hand. The person who doesn't know what is happening usually gets sacrificed.

COPING
WITH THE MISUSE
OF POWER

■ Probably the best way to avoid the trap with Little Big Horn is to know it's happening. Seeing it will help you avoid enlisting in a losing battle. You may eventually be able to sit back and watch the intricate play without concern for your own safety, providing you can follow the tone and process of the meetings.

■ Do not avoid tossing your own ideas in for discussion. You don't want to run the risk of poor job performance. There is also the danger of incurring resentment from those who have been bruised by, and survived, Little Big Horn.

■ If someone tries a Little Big Horn or Hedda Hopper then listen as politely as you can and try saying: "I guess you didn't like the idea I presented. Can you tell me what its weaknesses and strengths are?" This should serve to reduce the tension of the trap, or at least have it set for someone else far away from you.

■ Use your own behavior as a corrective force. When someone else speaks up, focus your criticism on the ideas expressed while simultaneously making positive comments about the person. Watch for too heavy a dose of patronization.

■ Good leaders measure and control the subtle line between attacking the idea and attacking the person presenting the idea. Adequate leaders know the difference between the two and feel responsible for not allowing personal attacks to occur.

■ On the other hand, good followers do not offer themselves up as scapegoats. Scapegoating occurs here when the idea presenter takes the criticism of the idea as a personal attack (or affront) even when it isn't. Both leaders and followers have the potential for adding to these confusions in work groups.

WELL, WHO IS THE MANAGER
WHO CAN HANDLE STRESS?

A manager is a person who works inside a group watching over tasks and feelings related to the group's work. This person sits at the edge, or boundary, of the group and monitors what comes into the group and what goes out of the group. All this happens with the manager having membership in two separate groups, each with its own separate tasks and conflicting assumptions. A manager works with, and belongs to, a group to get a job done, while also working with, and belonging to, another group of people also called managers. Managers, like their employees, have managers to whom they are accountable. Good managers have to be able to handle the conflict of simultaneous membership in the groups they manage, the group with all managers, and the group that manages them, too.

You can see how complex managing is when you begin to think about the kinds of distortions in task and communication that occur between two (or more) groups trying to get work done. It is all too easy for each of us to assume that a particular leader is behaving the way he or she is because of some character flaw or strength. It is much harder to study the myriad variables that impinge on management functions in work groups to come to the clearer (but not as simple) conclusion that what is happening derives not always from the personality of the manager, but possibly from the nature of the task.

A SUMMARY OF STRESSES
IN ORGANIZATIONS

The following vignette is a rich example of the dynamics covered in this chapter: groups, leadership, personal choice in the face of group pressure, broad goals and loyalties, administrative style, and the revealing of personal feelings.

OTHELLO

Art was the newly appointed chairman of a fourteen-person biology department whose teaching load was not different from the rest of the college. He was young for the position, carried good credentials, and did well at his previous job. He walked into his job with a department that had interim leadership for almost four years. Five of the fourteen employees were undertrained, overpaid, and underproductive. Three were openly hostile on his arrival. Twelve of fourteen employees had tenure.

Art quickly hired three new people, and then established six executive level committees (each with six members) to run the department. Each committee met for ninety minutes, once a week. There were committees for personnel, undergraduate education, postgraduate education, scientific activities, research, and general administration. He had ideas about "democratic leadership" so he refused to be chairperson of any of the committees. However, he did appoint himself secretary of every committee. It wasn't long before the secretary of the personnel committee was writing memos to the secretary of the research committee, and so on. Art had to control everything while presenting the illusion of democracy. Within a year he was irritable at work, little red veins began appearing on his cheeks, and he was forgetting more and more of the tasks he was allocating. Frequent arguments occurred with one of the staff members he had hired. Three times he became grossly intoxicated at department parties.

With six committees at ninety minutes per meeting, only seventeen members in the whole department, over 160 students to keep tabs on, there wasn't much time for the department members to get anything done. Art had no tolerance for those people who "couldn't cut it," yet he did nothing about those people who didn't. Most of the work fell on a few workaholics and idealists.

Art couldn't remember enough of what was being done to hold anyone consistently accountable. He had to increasingly rely on the mounds of internal departmental memos he was generating. Finally, his own competitive feelings led him to blame and argue with those people who were producing.

Meanwhile most of the department was silent. People were openly afraid of Art's tirades and irrational decisions. Two people wished "that he'd hang himself." One person suggested buying him a case of liquor and hoping he'd drink it all in one sitting.

One untenured faculty member that Art hired resigned from all his committee assignments with an open statement to the department that there was just too much time wasted administrating too few people. The rest of the department was silent, afraid of being attacked by Art. They could only resent the one person who acquired freedom. Art accused this person of attacking him by going behind his back to the Dean, trying to get him fired.

Art's mother was ill 1000 miles away, he was under a lot of stress and forgetting a lot more. Within six months Art fired this person, after bringing two members of his department to the Dean to describe how "sick" the fired person was. The Dean was confused by the data that had come to him about the firing. His own contact with the person had been professionally fruitful. On the other hand, one of the people (person A) who had come in with Art was trusted greatly by the Dean. The other person (B) was another of the young faculty that Art had hired. The Dean urged Art to back off and reconsider. Art refused. The firing was supported by the Dean because he felt it unwise to countermand one of his department chairman over an internal issue. Art continued his usual management style.

Three months later, person A retracted his "analysis" of Art. Now, he said it was Art who was not functioning, not the fired person. Soon thereafter, person B marched into the Dean's office suggesting that he be made the new department chairman. Two months later Art was asked to step down as department chairman. Person A was appointed the new chairman of the department. Person B left the department for another job. Art swapped jobs with his successor; and over the next years functioned fairly well in his nonleadership position. His drinking continued to worsen.

ANALYSIS
REVEALING PERSONALITY FLAWS ALWAYS SETS THE TERMINATION TRAP

The above description reveals many dynamics of leadership and followership. The complexity of the troubled manager is similar to a Shakespearean tragedy. This is the clearest of all traps; everyone's job is on the line. There is no good or bad, just ugly. Twisted leaders are both products of, and producers of, twisted institutions. It is as difficult for an employee to recognize that a leader is disturbed as it is for a child to recognize that a parent isn't doing well. Only a few characters can win, and they aren't always the most savory. Decisions, like those of the faculty member who quit the committees or the Dean, appear correct in one context and destructive in another. People adopt roles resembling vultures, others become the carrion, still others paying spectators. And the roles shift too quickly for goodness and fairness to win. Everybody would appear to lose something: be it the opportunity to work productively, a job, the enjoyment of a job well done, or, as in Art's case, health and sanity.

COPING
WITH THE DISTURBED LEADER

■ Remember that Othello, Desdimona, and Iago all lost something. Fallen leadership bodes poorly for all.

■ Consider riding out the storm as a worthwile mechanism for surviving the disturbed leader. Pull in, focus only on your own work, alienate no one. Speak only of work, be dumb or indifferent to the plight of the leader, and ride out the storm. This is good advice if you must keep your job. The price can be internalizing all the stress and disappointment.

■ Examine your own set of principles. If your job is expendable you can afford to consider how comfortable you will feel abdicating, versus retaining, your own set of principles. You work with them 40 hours per week and live with yourself outside of work another 128 hours.

■ The play Othello lasts for about four hours. Othello at work has no intermissions and can go on for years. Consider transfer or relocation before you subject yourself to the strain of the craziness, or the vengeance of a distorted mind and a potentially indifferent organization. There are times when it is fair to put your principles quietly in a suitcase and move on, before the trap snaps shut.

Certain factors, then, do impact on the nature of impersonal and personal forces in groups and their leadership. Increasing your awareness of the multilayered dynamics in every organization will lead to more understanding on your part of what becomes your work experience. The next chapter is filled with particular examples of work-related problems. Each example represents an expansion upon the dynamics discussed in the previous chapters.

CHAPTER

4

SAVING
YOUR JOB
FROM SET-UPS
THE TRAPS YOU CAN
MANEUVER AROUND

D
o you hear a cage rattling? Does anyone else smell the bait? Something is making you or other employees feel uncomfortable. It could be a Set-Up: a complex sequence of company actions that invites you to back yourself into a corner while the trap snaps shut.

With a Set-Up there is no decision to fire you. There's just an invitation to walk into the Termination Trap. If you accept the carefully hidden invitation, you can end up being fired. If you refuse the invitation too loudly (and expose the Set-Up) you could be labeled a troublemaker. But, if you can recognize the Set-Up and devise means to avoid or neutralize it, there is the possbility for saving your job. At the very least, you'll have more control over the when, where, and how of being fired.

A WAY OF LIFE
IN ORGANIZATIONS

Set-Ups are a way of life in organizations. A day doesn't go by without offering all the employees chances to get themselves fired. Work-life is filled with the risks and perils of being scapegoated, a most common form of Set-Up. It is a sad truth that people in groups are inclined to find someone to blame for the problems of the group. Simon, the young prophet in William Golding's novel, *Lord of the Flies*, goes out one night to find the monster in the lagoon that has frightened the other children. He returns the next morning to inform the group that the monster in the lagoon is "us." The children kill him for this. The message is: a group often wants to explain away its own problems by creating monsters (or scapegoats). Anyone who tries to interrupt this displacement of responsibility runs a terrible risk. This is one reason why it is risky to expose a Set-Up openly.

Set-Ups create the kind of unbearable stress and tension that can lead you to behave irrationally enough to jeopardize your job. Set-Ups are behaviors that come from other people that have the uncanny characteristic of being able to control your behavior. This control occurs because the Set-Up evokes a series of predictable reactions from you, especially if you don't recognize what is happening to you. This is the position of the scapegoat.

Scapegoats

In order to be scapegoated, two dynamics must occur in a group situation. First, forces exist in the group to single out individuals in order to place upon them negative, unwanted, or difficult feelings. Second, certain individuals in the group have to be willing to accept these negative projections of the group, and became the scapegoat. A person's willingess to be a scapegoat can be open and informed, with the attitude that "someone has to do this."

However, the willingness to be scapegoated can also occur beyond a person's awareness. The need to be sacrificed, or hurt, can be imbedded so deeply within the potential scapegoat's personality that he or she can't see it coming. We will focus on specific, painful dynamics that occur in work groups which can scapegoat a person.

In some of the discussion you will find events which relate directly to your own past experience. Other vignettes may seem distant, and not so applicable to your circumstance. Read them all carefully.

They are all common enough to have the potential for entering your life. Observe what does and can happen in work groups. You will be better able to understand and devise coping solutions for Set-Ups. You may not be able to change these dark and destructive forces in groups, but you can change your ability to cope with them by understanding just what they are all about.

First, though, you need to be able to recognize a Set-Up, even the tiny ones, so often veiled in an innocuous comment or memo. Then you'll want to become skilled in analyzing what is happening and developing appropriate coping procedures. Getting out of a Set-Up is a delicate art of nonconfrontation. Some people can get out of Set-Ups intuitively. Some of us need to study and understand them and to have ideas for coping with them long in advance. Here's an example of a Set-Up.

AMBULANCE

Jennifer had been working on the assembly line for only three months. Most of the other employees were older than she. The three oldest people began with the company the day it opened. Lunchtime was filled with angry talk about these three employees, and Jennifer already found it impossible to not jump in with her frustrations. The three eldest women always fell behind in their piecework, forcing everyone to slow down and lose money. It had gotten to the point where the rest of the line employees would decide each morning who would rescue the old folks. Jennifer, and everybody else, would spend two or three hours a week doing the other people's jobs just to keep things moving along.

This all seemed to happen with the shop manager's quiet approval. Though he never directly mentioned it, everyone was sure that he knew the three oldest employees were not functioning well. Jennifer also observed that there were two women on the line who never rescued the old folks. They were considered by the "ambulance crew" to be outsiders who only looked out for themselves. It occurred to Jennifer that these two women had worked at the plant longer than anyone else other than the three oldest women.

One hot summer afternoon, while helping one of the slow women speed things up, Jennifer screamed at her in frustration. The old woman started to cry. Jennifer was fired on the spot.

ANALYSIS

ALTRUISM CAN BE BUILT

UPON A TERMINATION TRAP

In order to understand the Ambulance you must first see that the "rescuer" is the "rescuee." Help is given to incompetent employees by those who feel their own job is in jeopardy because of the other people's incompetence. Ambulance is not played by those people who are helping out in a temporary situation. Ambulance is an ongoing problem.

The reward for the helping employee is two-fold. First, there is the belief in doing good for someone else. The self-righteousness often knows no bounds. It gives the "ambulance drivers" permission to talk and complain about those whom they are helping. Secondly, the employees feel they are protecting their jobs, or increasing their pay, or doing good for the company. It is also a quick way to feel like part of an in-group.

The reward for the manager of this situation (or the company) is getting the work done without having to fire incompetent people, an unpleasant task. The company also gets to believe that it rewards its loyal employees by keeping them at work even though they may have trouble functioning. It's always only a few token loyalists who survive. Everyone else gets too tired or frustrated and quits, or they are fired, before being there long enough to become loyalists themselves. One other benefit to the company is that it avoids developing consistent job performance appraisal systems. This is a difficult managerial task, and the criteria once developed may also be applied to the managers.

Remember that Ambulance is not infrequent in those situations where workers have seniority, especially where there are unions. There may be powerful forces exerted on you to help out some older, or chronically ill, person even though it's at your own expense.

COPING

WITH YOUR INCLINATION TO

HELP INCOMPETENT EMPLOYEES

■ Avoid driving an Ambulance, or being a patient in one. In either case there is a trap in the road ahead.

■ Know the difference between helping out someone in acute, infrequent trouble, and helping yourself by covering over someone's chronic incompetence.

■ Take the temporary risk of alienation from those employees who enjoy driving Ambulances. They won't keep their jobs for too long anyway. It takes too much time and energy away from their tasks. The major exception to this is when a person is hired specifically to rescue someone else. This person can be anything from a White House aid or press secretary to a secretary or "go-fer." Know what your job description is before you take the job!

■ Participate in company discussions which have to do with monitoring employee performance. Avoid discussing personalities. Focus only on defining the job and how to assess job performance. Participate in discussions about rewarding long-term employees with some form of job security that won't hold others back.

■ Share this experience with someone outside of work. The Judaeo-Christian traditions that will conflict with your not helping are powerful guilt inducers. You will need a lot of support here.

INITIAL CLUES
TO SET-UPS

All Set-Ups share one feature in common: something happens at work that gives the employee an uneasy, almost panicky, feeling inside that is often so strong it demands relief. How the employee goes about seeking relief from this feeling determines whether or not they grow, learn, and preserve their job, or end up scapegoating themselves right into termination. This feeling can be focused right at the source of the tension, or more usually just sits inside the person with its source unrecognized.

Recognizing the trapped feeling of a Set-Up gives you the opportunity to improve your work performance and relationships, even save your job. The way to avoid reacting destructively is to understand the nature and characteristics of the Set-Up and to initiate your own corrective behaviors.

MISUSE OF POWER

Every workplace, no matter how small, has to make and carry out decisions. Each person has a different amount of power to get things done. The things that get done often have too much to do with the personalities of the people, rather than the primary task of the company. The way things get done is also a function of the style of the people and the institution. One way a Set-Up can control you is through the misuse of the flow of power within the organization. The following examples clearly depict how the personality of a manager plus the organizational pressures on that manager come together and hurt subordinate employees.

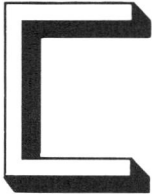

THE SHREDDED FEAT

A scientist fresh out of training spent six months working up an original research project at a large government research institute. Months of reading and writing ended with the director of her division complimenting her profusely. The director approved the project and sent it upwards into the bureaucracy for further approvals. Two months later the project came back with full approval and one striking change. The director was now listed as the principal investigator, and the young researcher was titled lab assistant. When confronted with the change, the director responded: "Well that's the way it is. You're messing with the big boys now!"

David was a long-term employee of a large novelty manufacturing company. He suggested a new way to package an old, poorly selling sport trophy. His suggestion was received with much enthusiasm. Three days later he got a standard corporate-wide memo informing him that "We have decided on repackaging the sport trophy in the following way . . ." David's idea was hidden in the "we." He never received formal credit for the product's improved sales record.

ANALYSIS

USE OF POWER TO ACQUIRE
VALUABLE EMPLOYEE RESOURCES

The nature of this transaction for employer and employee is power and the acquisition of valuable commodities for a minimal cost. Workable ideas and solutions are a valuable commodity in a competitive environment. The unstated goal is for certain individuals to gain the benefits from these ideas at the expense of others. Some young employees welcome Shredded Feat. It allows them to start early in their career doing important work that yields the credit for their work to the boss, while they get otherwise inaccessible experience, power, resources, and authority. They get to "use" the position of the boss without the burden of responsibility.

Occasionally the objective of Shredded Feat is a Rite of Passage. Each new employee pays dues to the organization by relinquishing one good idea (or solution) to someone else. In this case it happens to everyone, but just once; and the company quickly reveals the secret of the Rite to the person who doesn't overreact. Being a Rite of Passage doesn't excuse the fact that the someone else benefits from your ideas. What is critical here is that you don't overreact. Remember that this is a Set-Up, not an overt action to force you out. Your response will determine the course of events.

If the victim of Shredded Feat screams in pain he or she may discover there is no rescue. If others have suffered the same fate they may have lost their compassion or feel jealous of potential success. There is also no place for those who don't see the humor in a Rite of Passage. Complaining about the pain may result in early dismissal.

If you get angry, you invite the response of bewildered innocence from the culprit. Maybe it was a mistake, someone might unconvincingly suggest. If you're lucky your boss may just tell you you're "messing it up with the big boys." At least you'll know a few more rules for the next scrimmage. Getting angry also invites a label of deviance or troublemaking.

Feeling unrecognized and unrewarded for doing quality work is draining. It can be even worse if at the same time you are watching someone else reap the benefits of your work. It can feel as if no one recognizes you or your accomplishments. If your work slows down you invite the criticism of not producing. Your job is in jeopardy, but anyone sensitive to the issues (like the person who robbed you of credit) won't have trouble relating the onset of your poor work performance to the event that is draining you.

It may be true that it is your idea, but you don't expect anyone to believe you, do you? Unless we're talking patentable material with you holding the notorized papers, there's big trouble for you if you claim ownership. It's too much sour grapes. Do you expect people to admit publicly that they robbed your idea? It becomes your word against theirs; and if they had enough authority to write a distorted memo in the first place, their memory is big enough to have your job.

COPING
WITH THE LOSS OF YOUR
IDEAS OR HARD WORK

■ Keep the memo that documents your Shredded Feat. If no memo exists (if it were an announcement, for example), write down what was said.

■ Write a memo of record and date it. Put down everything you can remember about your idea: why you came up with it (was it an assigned task or something done on your own initiative); how you came to that solution; and to whom you presented the idea. Be specific about names, places, and times.

■ File all the above in a personal place. You should gain solace from knowing that you are keeping track of the first event. It might be worthwhile to casually ask a friend if this ever happened to him or her, but be careful not to divulge your reason for inquiring. Try to find out if this is a usual event. Collect data.

■ Review the general process you use to share your creative ideas. Is there any chance you are not asserting yourself firmly enough? Do you use indefinite pronouns when you really mean "I"? Do you try to share your glory for good reasons (and then later forget your intent)?

■ Is there any chance what you remember as your idea really wasn't? Many ideas do come from "we" and "us" in that creativity is a multistep process. Remember, nothing could be more dangerous then documenting and presenting your side of everything only to discover other coworkers have evidence of their involvement with the idea.

■ If you present a creative idea in a meeting, and the idea gets a favorable response, write a follow-up memo (immediately) elaborating on your idea and note all who were present at the meeting. As a matter of course, send copy memos to at least two people to protect your ideas. This latter recommendation should be followed only in those circumstances where ideas have already been taken away from their creators. To instigate this move prior to that time will foster an environment of suspiciousness which may only call undue attention to your not being a team player.

■ If it happens again, go through the same procedure in the above three steps. Consider presenting your data to the inaccurate memo writer in a gentle style. The best approach is "Gee, I think someone forgot how this idea evolved." And "Here are some notes I have taken about those meetings." Don't be alarmed or disappointed by a seeming nonrecognition of your efforts in documenting. Do not expect anyone to back down. You are only going on subtle record as being willing to document what has transpired. What has been suggested should make most of the problem go away forever. It means you have lost two good career milestones that someone else has taken credit for, but you have learned how to respond in your best interests to a Set-Up.

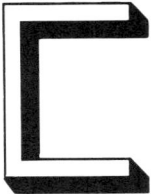

MUSH AND GRITS

Three times in two weeks Fred's manager raked him over the coals for not finishing a particular graphics project. It was a busy ad agency, and Fred just couldn't remember being told to do the project. He remembered the meetings where the projects were discussed, but the work had not been assigned to him or to the three other artists on the full-time payroll. In fact, he finally protested to his boss; he was pretty sure his boss had mentioned something about doing the work himself. This was denied (in spite of the fact that Fred had checked with others to be sure they remembered it the way he did). Fred was in a quandary, and he didn't let it go. He registered his complaint with the agency's owner. Two weeks later there was no Christmas bonus. By March he was let go with the explanation there wasn't enough work for him.

ANALYSIS
POWER CAN BE USED TO DIFFUSE
AUTHORITY AND RESPONSIBILITY

In Mush and Grits there is a manager who hides his incompetence by benefitting from assigning work in a very amorphous fashion. It is never quite clear who is to do the work, how it is to be done, and when it is to be finished. When the project is due, the results are evaluated by this same manager. Then, because of the initial lack of clarity, he or she can take credit for all the good work and give the criticism away to the underlings. This interaction can also be played out between people at the same administrative level when they don't work out boundaries between themselves on a mutually shared task. On any level, it is an insidious form of Set-Up. You will need to be aware of it in order to survive in your work environment.

A variation of Mush and Grits is Shoots and Ladders. This resembles the childhood board game of similar name. It occurs when your boss encourages your subordinates to climb a ladder right over you and go directly to him without seeing you first. Decisions are made when these two levels communicate without you, and you are then "shot" for any errors that occur. As time goes on your ladder of influence gets shorter and shorter as your job gets undermined.

On another level Mush and Grits is a transaction of competing inferiorities. The person who assigns the mush, the poorly defined work task, lacks the ability to present expectations in a clear manner. Certainly the mush assigner knows what quality work is; whenever the job is done well, he takes the credit for it. In order for a manager to behave this way, there have to be people who feel unsure enough about themselves to be willing to accept the mush to work on, as well as the gritty anger afterwards when, or if, things go wrong.

COPING

WITH DOING WORK WITHOUT
CLEAR AUTHORITY AND RESPONSIBILITY

■ Anytime you accept work without clear authority and responsibility, you are putting your job on the line. When you accept a task where the boundaries of the task, the resources to accomplish the task, the criteria for assessing the outcome and its quality, and the time of completion are not clearly defined, there is a serious risk to your status at work. We all have to do this in our work sometimes. Keep clear in your mind just how much authority and responsibility you have. Ninety-five percent of the experience of any kind of pain is determined by a person's psychological state. If you see it coming you can at least avoid being surprised by the pain.

■ Carry a pad of paper and pen to all meetings whether you are alone or in a group. When work is assigned off the record, without formal memo or assignment, politely ask your boss to repeat what was said. Write it down. If you feel there's a chance that either you're supposed to do the work, or you'll get blamed for it being done poorly even though someone else may do it, read back to your boss and/or the group what you've written down. This reading should be prefaced with a request for help. You want people to tell you if what you wrote down was accurate. After the reading if things aren't suddenly clarified by the purveyor of mush, it then becomes fair game to ask a few simple questions. What are the boundaries of the task? What are the human and physical resources allocated to the task? What are the criteria for assessing outcome and quality? What is the time of completion?

There is the reasonable hope that your behavior might structure your boss right out of the destructive behaviors. Remember to keep very cool, and do not talk with anyone else about doing this. As constructive as your behavior might be, those who are less sure of themselves or jealous of you might see your actions as plotting. That is a sure way to get scapegoated.

■ You really can't avoid poorly assigned work. Do not try to control something that is beyond your sphere of influence, especially if you want to keep your job. You can keep records of the work you do, however. Your note pad or memos of record should remind you (and maybe others) exactly what was said. This can be useful behind closed doors in the boss's office, especially if you use it very gently and only as a reminder that you don't feel you deserve the grits being served to you.

■ Always consider transfer. Any manager or boss who behaves this way is on a sinking ship. There just aren't a whole lot of people who behave this way in successful enterprises. One day something is going to catch up to this person. Knowing your outside options, without even exercising them, can be great solace.

ROBOT

Harry worked in a state geological survey office right after getting his Ph.D. He was hired to do detailed county maps of the entire state which located all of the mineral and petroleum reserves. Each day his boss would come and tell him which county to work on. Harry was anxious to do well on his first job, so at first his boss's suggestions were very helpful. It freed Harry from having to exercise his own judgments about scheduling the work. Harry made it a point to visit each county to verify the exact location of the mineral and petrochemical reserves. After a while, Harry had enough experience to determine what needed to be finished and when. In addition there were some projects that Harry enjoyed more than others, and his boss's directions did not take that into account.

Eight months into the job, the first completed county maps returned from the printers. Harry was shocked to see his boss's name

listed as the creator of the map. His own name was nowhere to be seen. His boss, though a geologist, had done none of the research or cartography and was a full twenty years removed from an in-the-field geological survey.

When confronted, the boss reminded Harry that he had assigned all the work and directed the progress. He emphasized that Harry must have known he did not have enough experience to get the job done without this form of direction. Harry pointed out to him that he had repeatedly sent signals that he didn't want the direction. The boss reported receiving none of them. The impasse was unresolvable. Harry checked back to discover all the maps done by the geological survey in the past twenty-eight years had his boss's name on them. He also discovered that his position had been refilled every two to three years.

ANALYSIS
THE USE OF POWER
TO EXPLOIT

Robot is also very similar to Shredded Feat. This is a Set-Up because the employee is willing to be a robot, totally controlled and given no credit for quality work when the job situation is stable. Only when the person feels dissatisfied do things become unstable. The mechanism is exploitation. The excuse given for treating people as robots is they "can't think for themselves," or "you can't trust an employee to perform on schedule, or with enough quality." The real reason is exploitation of other people's success.

Although the consequences are similar to Shredded Feat and Mush and Grits, Robot creators are different. They have to control people's behaviors. Maybe it's their own need to have perfection, their own tension about work performance, or maybe a difficulty sharing the limelight. No matter the reason, they have to be in control.

There is a secret payoff for the employee. Those people who like freedom from having to schedule their own work and freedom from being responsible for the quality of their work find the Robot is an excellent role to adopt. Many people elect to be Robots. Robot is made easier by the fact that the Robot-maker rarely blames the Robot for mistakes (as in Mush and Grits). Robot-makers need to control everything and generally have no trouble with carrying responsibility too. Some Robot-makers are like Gepetto. They appreciate their puppets, know they are doing a fine job, and, in addition, pay them higher than usual salaries to stay in their place.

COPING

WITH BEING UNDER
SOMEONE ELSE'S CONTROL

■ Know before you take the job or assignment just how well your boss can delegate authority along with responsibility. This can be done by asking to meet with other people who have worked under and above your boss. In many companies it is standard practice to have these interviews. Look closely at your interview for tiny behavioral clues about the organizational styles. Are the people you meet punctual or late for your meeting, unusually neat or casual, responders or initiators, humorful or bland? Many opposites can be chosen for this analysis, but be sure to pick those qualities that fit with your style of working.

■ Be sure your boss's ability to delegate fits with your work style. When your boss is appointed after you are on the job, Robot is harder to solve. But being aware of what is going on will help while you decide what your next step will be.

■ Regularly suggest to your boss tasks that need doing. Given that the issue is control (and not making you look as bad as it feels), if you provide the structure and at the same time put your boss in control, then you become more the master of your own fate. This is not easy to do if the person you are dealing with is so bent on being in control that he or she will not go along with your excellent (be sure they are at least that) suggestions simply because they are *your* suggestions.

■ If there is any chance that you have gone along with being a robot for a period of time, it is distinctly unfair to whine or cry about it or to be angry. This is not playing fair and can result in a quick firing. If you want to keep your job and stop being a robot, you must proceed slowly and diplomatically.

■ If the position becomes untenable for you, this is one of those times to keep very quiet (to preserve a good job recommendation) and start looking around. It's best, if you feel your insides burning, to consider employment elsewhere, before you either burn-out or get too angry to do your job well. An outside possibility is to approach management to change your job description. If this doesn't help the way you get work assignments, at least it might benefit your successor (should you leave).

CASTOR OIL AND DEFOLIATION

These are the unusually common situations where you are assigned work that your boss already knows you don't like doing (Caster Oil) or you are removed from a key committee or work assignment (Defoliation). It is usually presented on a silver platter and therefore resembles a Smorgasbord. In a Smorgasbord the offering looks and tastes appealing. In Caster Oil you are asked to do something that is dressed up to look appealing; often your boss will imply that doing it is for your own good. In Defoliation you are given similar messages along with gentle reassurances that "everything will be just fine," or "you really won't be missing anything," or "that committee is a real waste of time, anyhow."

These situations are always Set-Ups. It is very difficult, however, to know whether or not Caster Oil is a malicious undermining of your morale or just one of the many times in life when somebody has to do something they do not want to do. If the assignment represents one of those many unwanted tasks that just has to get done, complaining or dragging your feet will only serve to alienate you from your boss as well as your fellow employees. If you resist, some people can dump a load of self-righteousness on you and you won't ever be forgiven.

Defoliation has darker overtones to it. Assuming there is an intended demoralization or humiliation, it is dangerous to complain or stall. This plays right into the perpetrator's hands. Suddenly your boss can appear ashamed of you, or surprised, or disappointed. Then comes that clear sense you will never be forgiven. You won't; that's what the interaction is all about. You will have fallen for the Set-Up.

To cope with this sort of Set-Up and not fall for the trap, close your eyes, hold your nose, and take the unwanted job assignment. Never complain or moan to anyone. It invites a progression of Set-Ups. You can keep a private tally of the frequency of those kind of assignments to check the fairness of the job distribution.

If the allocations are predictably unfair, or if one job is noticeably crushing to you, consider opening the discussion further. You might try inquiring about the limits of the task: its due date and who will supply any needed raw materials or technical support. Be sure to review whether you have the special expertise to do this particular task.

Watch your boss for tiny facial and body signals or special voice intonations to detect an intentional Set-Up.

If your boss asks if there is a problem for you in doing the task, your response should be something like: "No, although I'm not particularly excited about doing this project, I do understand that there are pressures on you to get this done. I am more than willing to carry my fair share." No need to translate the intent of this message to anyone. If your boss is callous to it in the future, then either management is coming down too hard on your boss (and he or she is passing it on to you), or your boss is originating a Set-Up just for your benefit.

Consider transfer or a new job if the volume or frequency of Caster Oil doesn't ease up. If you are trapped in the job for financial or personal reasons, then change Caster Oil into Eagle Scout. Use your survival skills and dig in. Sometimes weathering the storm earns huge numbers of merit badges plus sympathy. Both are potential liquid assets at work.

Stay very cool and monitor your performance. Defoliation could well be a signal of getting fired, but don't assume you are going to lose your job for sure. Search out adequate feedback (without whining about the lost assignment) concerning your performance. There is also the possibility that you are not really needed on that task anymore. Check that out. It might be that someone did you a favor, even though you feel slighted.

SEDUCTION AND COMPROMISE

The next series of Set-Ups are ones that control your behavior by seducing you into a compromised position which renders you less competent to get your job done. In all cases the seduction is a direct appeal to your personal needs or insecurities. Sometimes companies will be run in such a way to render people more vulnerable to getting seduced. For example, there may be few public acknowledgments of a job well done. This may leave some people hungry for recognition and support. When it comes, even in damaging forms, the recipient still takes it and ends up getting hurt. This is the case in our first example.

THE SUCKERBALL

In the last four long range planning sessions with all the managers in her division, Rosalie found herself answering questions for which she had no special knowledge. The first two times she was asked, it was a simple: "Isn't that right, Rosalie?" Of course it was her boss asking the question, so the safest thing to do was just agree. The problem was that she was being asked to confirm a marketing decision, and Rosalie worked in product development. The third time her boss asked her to give an opinion on future buying trends. The question came so gently that her answer just flowed out, based entirely on intuition. She had no data or experience to support her conclusion.

The fourth question was more of a request. Her boss asked her to prepare a report on ways to enhance quality control in the manufacturing process for the next meeting. It seemed logical, Rosalie did know all about inventing and developing things, and she was being asked to look at developing a new idea.

It didn't occur to Rosalie how over her head she was until 3 A.M. the next morning. She woke up in a cold sweat with a tight feeling in her chest. Rosalie worried about having a heart attack until she began realizing what had happened at work. Her husband sat with her for the next two hours sorting through her tensions and worries. Rosalie decided that she had to finish the project she had agreed to do, even though her tension came from her lack of experience to handle the assignment. She had swung at a suckerball. She had to make the best of her own mistake; it was too late to turn back.

Peter, on the other hand, knew that he wanted to please his boss. They seemed to like one another. Many times his boss would come into his sales booth and ask his advice about things that seemed important to new car sales. Peter had an opinion about most everything. Selling automobiles was a very competitive business. Always there were pressures to produce more sales. If it wasn't an incentive program, there were deadlines. Recognition was sporadic, so any time a sales meeting came around and Peter was asked to express his opinion, he felt complimented. No matter that he knew almost nothing about what he was expounding upon. At least he felt recognized and respected in front of the other salesmen.

Once his boss asked Peter what he thought would make a difference in used car sales. Peter gave a ten minute answer. When he finished, the manager of used car sales pointed out in a tense, gravel voice that Peter had never set foot on the used car lot. He had never sold a used car, continued the gravel voice, and was third to the last in new car sales for the last three months. Peter felt wounded then, and again in one month when he was fired "for shooting off his mouth in meetings."

ANALYSIS
SEDUCTION USED
TO HUMILIATE

Suckerball is very similar to a nonwork dilemma: seduction. The lead-in is an inflation of your sense of importance. Suckerball does not occur in those situations where you do know the answer. It also is not part of the problem when the questioner knows neither the answer nor the correct person to get the answer from. When the boss asks you a question in front of others it can, if you're not careful, feel like a compliment. You should always remember that people ask questions of people who don't know the answer in order to not get the right answer. Read that again. If the one who asked the question wanted the right answer, he or she would ask someone who had the knowledge and experience. Getting the wrong answer in public may help solidify the boss's position in two ways. It makes his or her own answers look better or more solid. It also may serve to humiliate someone else for a change. However, if your boss doesn't know the right answer either, giving the wrong answer creates bigger problems. It exposes weaknesses in you and your boss. This is very dangerous, especially if your boss trusted you before you gave a wrong answer while pretending you knew something about what was asked. Then you've really been set up for a double whammy Suckerball.

COPING

WITH A

SEDUCTIVE REQUEST

■ Remember, if someone asks your opinion on a matter you know little about, do not ever give an answer. On the other hand you do not want to appear defensive. Respond by saying: "I don't know. If you want to give me some time I can ask . . ." You can also try: "I don't know, but with proper time I can adopt the following approach to find the answer." What the person may really want is the wrong, or ill-informed, answer. If you answer the question directly you may have given them what they want, but at your professional expense. And, if they knew enough to ask the question, they'll know an inadequate answer if you give it to them. If you defer, and say you don't know, then you expose your ignorance. You may then feel like you are in a no-win situation.

■ Tell the person it is an interesting question (which gives them some kind of reward, in case they are looking for that).

■ Inquire gently as to the reason for asking you the question. Do they have something in mind? What kind of answer do they expect?

■ If the above has not defused the request, the next step is to remind that person what your areas of expertise are and that your abilities give you no special talent in answering this important question. On the other hand, it is fair to suggest who in the company you feel could answer the question. If the person is in the room with you, there is the immediate opportunity to deflect the question over with "That's a really good question, maybe Xavier could answer it."

■ If there is no way to avoid giving an answer it is fair to proceed, but with caution. Preface your response with an acknowledgement of being asked, a clear statement that your response is only opinion, and that you hope the listener(s) take it as a naive outside view. Be careful to mention that sometimes an outside naive view can be fresh, or helpful, but that you don't expect to be that lucky. Give your answer. Then repeat again your hesitancy about making too much of your response, except that it is the best you can give from your perspective. This may all sound very long-winded, but it necessarily establishes you as a clear thinker, respectfully cautious, yet still willing to take some risks. It also avoids the trap of pitting you against your peers, or those people within the company who are informed in the area about which you stated your opinion.

THE SWIFT SHUFFLE

Alexander had spent twenty successful years designing sophisticated military weapons systems for a large mid-Atlantic state corporation. Then the head of his particular research division moved on. The replacement was young, energetic, and very competitive. He didn't seem to have much time for Alexander or his research ideas. For the first time work didn't seem very pleasurable.

One day his boss called Alexander into his office, shut the door, and asked to be shown the new trigger mechanism Alex had been working on. For three hours Alexander taught his boss everything about this new, untested device. There were years of confident design experience in each decision that Alex presented. Then the boss revealed a new weapon in need of Alex's trigger mechanism; but, he doubted the use of a particular timing device in Alexander's trigger design. Again Alex provided a detailed explanation of the benefits of that timing device and how it was an essential component in that triggering mechanism. The meeting closed with his boss supporting Alex fully and assuring him that the new weapon and Alex's trigger would fit nicely together. Alex felt a warm glow.

For the next two weeks Alex relaxed at work. At the end of two weeks the formal plans for the weapon were circulated to the appropriate design teams. There was Alex's basic trigger mechanism, but inside of it was his boss's timing device. The entire trigger device was credited to Alex. He kept his disappointment to himself; he did not have confidence in the timing device change.

Then the weapon's test failed four times, and the failure was attributed to the triggering device. Three times Alexander asked to rebuild the trigger. He wanted to use his own timing device. Each time his boss refused. He felt trapped. Eventually the company chose another complete triggering mechanism. Alexander was transferred to a do-nothing position as a result of three poor work appraisals. Each stated that he was stubborn, slow-moving, and unable to correct his own design flaws. Within one week of his transfer, Alexander's position was filled by the engineer who not only designed the accepted trigger mechanism, but who had also been a classmate of Alexander's boss in engineering school. Alexander left work within eighteen months following a long depression and heart attack.

ANALYSIS
SEDUCTION IS A QUICK
MEANS TO MANIPULATE

The Swift Shuffle is a common institutional trap. It usually occurs because someone in power is committed to an idea, but afraid to take responsibility for it. This makes it difficult for the person whose idea or plan has been shuffled to clarify the issue or confront the shuffler. After all, credit has been given. In the example given, there are intimations of some evil intent, or at the very least something feels wrong. The trap was set for Alexander when his idea was changed. But the baiting didn't start until the manager wished for him to leave. This Set-Up may be very difficult to maneuver around, but understanding what is happening can save a lot of emotional and physical stress.

COPING
WITH HARD-TO-GRASP
DECISION-MAKING

■ Take notes. Any time you are faced with a decision made in private, and there is even the slightest sense of distrust, it is fair to have some documentation of the event. That means you should carry a small notebook at all times. Write down decisions or events that impinge on your job. Date them and note the significant people present when the decision was made. It helps to read what you've written down to the other person(s). This gets around any feelings of distrust or suspiciousness about what you have been writing. Really all you are doing is quite appropriately work-related. It is fair to ask for a memo, or to inform those present you will send them a brief note documenting the meeting. If only one person is present consider sending copies to others "to keep them informed." Do it within twenty-four hours; keep a copy for yourself.

Keeping records like this in a candid, open fashion will gain the respect of some, the cautiousness of others, and some criticism from that group of people who don't want you to do it because it interferes with their modi operandi. There will also be a group who may resent your strict adherence to the tasks at hand. But don't assume that everyone is jealous. Those kinds of assumptions are self-made Set-Ups.

■ There are times when it is worthwhile to publicly announce that "somehow" your idea has been changed. This can be done with enough style and grace to be its own kind of Shuffle. The idea is to acknowledge what part of the system is your idea and what part isn't. In the same breath you want to be sure to give lots of credit to the new idea and its creator. Even though that new idea may be blatantly horrible to you, remember you have already been attacked once by the Swift Shuffle when someone else's idea was credited to you. You should divert further attacks with your smooth ingratiating manner. If everyone else knows the new idea is bad, you will get points for your diplomacy. If the idea ends up successful you get the same points for not having taken credit for it. Think how much better Alexander would have fared had he taken this approach.

■ Do not continue the Swift Shuffle by pretending it didn't happen. On every level there is a trap here that will eventually ensnare you. Find some way, if it can't be done openly in the company, to bring the change to someone's attention before events take place. Always use a gentle supportive approach to the Swift Shuffler.

■ Let someone else find out what the motives were. Make no statements about the other person's character (avoid trying to deal with the seductive quality of the Swift Shuffler by hurting someone else).

PLANTATION
OR
TENANT FARMER

Alice had spent six of the last nine weeks traveling for the company. Crisscrossing the country, she arranged two complex exchanges of technical information between her company and a competitor. She arrived back at the office just three days before her vacation to Puerto Rico.

Her boss congratulated her on the success of her trip. He then quickly notified her that she had to leave for a liaison trip to corporate headquarters to file an in-person report. Alice protested. She had planned a vacation. Her boss furrowed his brow into his well-known no-compromise signal and told her that he had rescheduled her vacation while she was gone. No one else could make the trip to headquarters but her, he told her. She was indispensable to him. Crestfallen, she meekly gave in to the compliment. It did inflate her ego and marked the beginning of what was to become a chronic problem of total workaholism.

Alice's annual work appraisals were super, her raises were 15 percent above the cost of living index, and Alice missed three subsequent vacations for similar reasons. Each time she let it hurt her a little bit less. Four years later, having accumulated almost ten weeks of vacation and three months of sick leave, Alice experienced a prolonged hospitalization and recuperation for an atypical severe arthritis. She quit work soon thereafter, tired and depressed.

ANALYSIS
SEDUCTION AS A FORM OF
HUMILIATION AND DENIGRATION

It is necessary to recognize the Plantation before you become enslaved or sick. The requests to do important work seem so legitimate and flattering that it can be hard for you to see how self-destructive your compliance is. First the company figures out a way to make you feel indispensable. Once you believe in your own indispensability, the company gets free work with fewer interruptions.

This often occurs in high-energy jobs like police work, banking, stocks and bonds, medicine, and advancing technology development and manufacture. The high raises and significant advancements up the corporate ladder are further rewards for your servitude. Yet, it is totally impossible to measure the worth of quiet private time to recharge your batteries. Besides, often the raises in salaries do not fairly compensate for the two to three week loss in time off.

Sometimes Tenant Farmer is used to force a marginally competent employee to leave. This is done by first putting the employee on probation and then demanding an immense amount of work. If the employee's productivity goes up everyone benefits, except the Tenant Farmer. The excessive work is tiring, and the percentage of the yield is usually very low. Should the employee survive the demands of probation, the next evaluation period's crop demands are often higher. The company can easily fire a Tenant Farmer and then figure out who's to be appointed next.

Ironically, the company's plantation masters usually deny personal freedom to those people who they think *are* dispensable. That's why it's so much of a Set-Up. If they don't think enough of you to value your personal freedom, then be wary. They consider you expendable (or consumable). Certainly it is true that some companies consume their human resources in order to compete effectively. But if you really are indispensable, if your personal freedom is usurped, you can only lose. You can count on the fact that corporate presidents and owners take most of the time they need to feel good about coming into work.

Remember that one of the most powerful effects of life on the Plantation is how it can erode your personal life. Slaves don't have a lot of control over their personal lives. It isn't just you who will miss that vacation, but there may be disappointment for the person(s) with whom you planned to go. Thus you end up squeezed between two conflicting forces: work and your personal life. If you are not careful, both can end up rejecting you, or you may get too sick and tired to function. This interaction has a lethal component to it.

COPING
WITH THE LIFE
OF A SLAVE

■ Let this happen only once in your career. Once allows for the possibility that Plantation may not be what you are experiencing.

■ Be careful to gently tell your boss that you are disappointed about your vacation delay, but you do understand things like this can happen. Do not complain. You want to avoid appearing disloyal to the organization.

■ Register as little show of emotion as possible. The more neutral you are, the more everyone can wonder about your feelings. This wonderment is to your advantage. Their not knowing where you stand gives you some leverage and control over your own circumstances.

■ Be especially careful to not allow your disappointment to interfere with the quality of your work, which won't be easy. If you do fall down on the task this one time, there can be a lot of ammunition to be used against you in future episodes of Plantation.

■ Ask your spouse or friend for special understanding when you cancel this one (and only) vacation. Unless your spouse works where you do, you cannot expect him or her to understand the special forces acting on you at this time. An apology plus the promise to never allow it to happen again is in order. Give that promise. It will help your relationship, *and* it might save your health and life. This recommendation is most important for those people who are Type A personalities (see p. 166).

WITHHOLDING

A company can control your behavior by withholding material possessions, information, or gratifying feelings. Withholding creates a sense of deprivation and want, which invariably leads to an increase in tension and uncertainty. A person who does not see the deprivation often begins to respond to the unmet needs by behaving in a way to make up for the company deprivations. Being acquisitive in a group situation by going after necessary rewards that are being held back can appear outwardly self-serving to others in the company who have "adjusted" to their own similar deprivations. These people may react to you in anger, out of jealousy, with accusations that you are too demanding. That is where the Set-Up begins.

SCHWINN
WITHHOLDING
BENEFITS
AS A WAY
TO ECONOMIZE

If you have always gotten a company car, and this year the make and model allotted to you is a clear step down the social ladder, you may be receiving a true signal your job is over—especially if you're the only person moving into a used car, two-wheeler, or no-wheeler.

On the other hand, this could be a clear reflection of unpleasant economic reality. It is always remotely possible that the problem could be a manager with poor taste in cars. Most likely, it is a clear signal of unfavorable feelings toward you coming from somewhere high up in the company.

If you are faced with this situation, do not complain, no matter what the causes are for Schwinn. If you are the only one getting a two-wheeler this year, take the message to heart. Some time later, clearly removed from the time of the vehicle assignments, approach your boss and ask what difficulties there have been with you or your work performance. If your boss asks what the request is all about, explain that you are working on making changes to be more beneficial to the company. Make no mention of vehicle assignments.

Taking the initiative is the one hope you have to divert getting fired. This may force some rethinking about your position. Even if there were no intentions to signal that you were in disfavor, asking for this appraisal (and acting favorably on it) still establishes your willingness to deal with bettering yourself and taking criticism usefully.

For the most part, however, Schwinn happens to everyone and only rarely is it a signal that your job is in jeopardy. What you want to avoid is over reacting because you feel hurt or wounded by the lack of prestige.

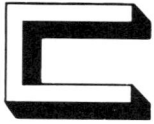

OUT TO LUNCH

There were two important publishing deadlines in the past week that couldn't be met because Harry's boss was just not returning his calls and messages. Harry was on time with his editing of the manuscript, and he felt pressure to get the work done. Urging his boss's secretary produced nothing. Repeatedly he went to the office only to be put off. More troublesome was Harry's knowledge that his boss was at work. Once he was there to get an appointment and his boss rushed passed him with the briefest hello. Harry felt tense and irritable. The production department was hounding him to pass the manuscript on.

ANALYSIS

WITHHOLDING CONTACT
IN ORDER TO HUMILIATE

Not getting a prompt reply from your boss is, at first glance, a seemingly harmless event. Everyone knows how busy the other person always is. In fact, the lack of response to a work-related communication has far reaching implications. One can never be sure if it is the employee or the boss who is out to lunch. There is a signal here; but a first glance does not locate the problem. It feels like a rebuff to the employee; if it is intended that way, it is a very powerful and humiliating tool. Anger can often be expressed by pulling away. In some organizations it's called Excommunication.

If this is not an intended rebuff, then your boss is either overworked, under some time-limited unusual personal or professional pressure, or not functioning well.

COPING

WITH ISOLATION
FROM YOUR BOSS

■ First determine from neutral questioning of other employees whether or not this is the boss's usual behavior.

■ If the answer is yes, then be cautious about not stressing your boss further. On the other hand you cannot lose sight of the importance of your own project. Consequently it is important to continue leaving specific messages. Each message should be increasingly detailed, outlining what it is you need. Be openly sensitive to your boss's pressures. If you aren't, you can turn a usual event into a Set-Up for your own career.

■ If this seems to be a long-standing behavior on your boss's part, then continue to leave specific messages. Additionally, make an appointment with your boss's superior. It might be worth while to mention in one of your messages to your own boss that you are going to do this "for the sake of keeping your project moving." In the appointment with your boss's superior, present only your dilemma and the fact that your boss seems very busy. If your work situation is more desperate, then consider bringing up the possibility that maybe there is something wrong with your work that is causing your boss to avoid you. If that is the case then you would like to know about it. Do not underestimate anyone else's ability to read between your lines. There is no reason to state your case any more clearly than this.

■ If you are certain your boss is behaving this way only with you, then continue to try to clarify the problem in a calm straightforward way. Try meeting with your boss and openly discussing the problem. If that fails, then consider carefully the consequences of approaching your boss's boss with the specifics of your being singled out. The outcome depends on the administrative tone and style in your company (whether or not there is an open door policy, for example). Remember that your boss's boss may have no idea there is a problem between you and your boss. Go prepared with memos, work sheets, progress reports, and documentation of your completing your work. Have it all in briefcase, neat and orderly. If you feel your boss is inclined to throw unsubstantiated allegations, do not defend yourself personally. Simply pull out material relevant to dealing with that topic and present your side of all the issues in a clear, concise manner. If the allegations are substantive, it is best to be open and honest. There are times when admitting the case against you is the first step to healing wounds. And if the wounds are not healable, at least you set the tone for your switching jobs or leaving the company. Avoid presenting yourself as downtrodden or victimized. These are two obvious shams which will only weaken your own case.

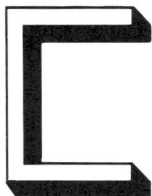

THE NIT
WITHHOLDING
INFORMAL FREEDOMS
IN ORDER TO CONTROL

Has a recent critique of your work performance included a selective enforcement of company policy? Have you been criticized for taking too long a lunch break when everyone else takes as long a break? Have you been criticized for getting to work late, or leaving too early, when, again, everyone else does? Are the criticisms related to matters that are clearly established in the company personnel manual, yet never enforced? Does your intellect tell you the issue is absolutely ridiculous, while some vague pressure builds in your head, throat, chest, or stomach? This is the clue that a trap has been set. These are just a very few examples of the Nit.

The Set-Up here is direct and to the point. Someone else has the authority to tell you what to do, and he or she is backed up by the company. It may be a simple power trip: an insecure or threatened manager playing checkers with your head, heart, and career. It could be that this person wants your dissatisfaction with the job to increase. It's possible that the company has decided to alter its enforcement of the rules and you were the first one approached (pretty rare). It's possible that someone above your boss has flown a nit at your boss; and now it's been passed on to you. One common nit is to create an aura of a problem that doesn't even exist. People will actually pretend anger as a managerial style to get others to back off and give in.

If you complain, argue, or come on strong with resentment then you open yourself up for getting fired. Your boss can get openly angry and hostile with you; your personnel file can fill up with specific criticisms about your responses to authority; and, you invite someone to consider how nice it might be to not have you around.

If you are in the wrong, or have transgressed a company rule, admit it openly and thoroughly. Ask what brings up enforcing the rule now. Watch your tone of voice here. You want to avoid implying anything indirectly. If the answer is that the company has decided to enforce it for everyone, then watch everyone for the next month to see if things change. Do not tattle on others or complain in any way. If the answer is that your boss feels he or she has been too lax with his or her employees, then watch them to see if they are influenced by changes for which you are being held accountable.

If your boss implies that he or she has been too lax with you, ask what it is you have done or have not done to bring this special attention. Listen carefully here, don't shut out what might be said. There could be early clues that you have not been meeting up in other areas.

If your boss directs criticism straightaway toward you, then consider this an early warning signal that your job is in jeopardy. Best to ask if this is so right away. The subsequent stages are far more painful than being nitted. Try and begin a dialogue about the major problem areas in your work performance immediately. Remember that when people become angry *at* you that doesn't always mean they are angry *with* you. We have trouble separating disagreeing with an idea from disagreeing with the person presenting the idea. Knowing this difference takes clear thinking, but it's worth striving toward.

NO ROOM FOR FEELINGS

Revealing personal feelings by speaking or acting poses certain dilemmas. There should be more then a little room for the heart at work. However, what should be and what is are often two different issues. Each work place has a different tolerance for personal expression in the context of carrying out work. Each person has to figure out where the traps are.

BABBLING BROOK

Harriet's pastrami sandwich kept sticking in her throat as she sat listening to her boss badmouth two other engineers. Many of the criticisms coincided with Harriet's impressions of her two peers, yet something made that pastrami too big to swallow.

That evening, for the first time in three years, Harriet got drunk before dinner. She yelled at the kids and ended up sleeping on the couch after an argument with her husband.

The next day her manager once more unloaded specific complaints about other employees. Then he mentioned how some of them didn't like Harriet. Again Harriet listened and remained silent as before. Three weeks later, Ed, a friend at work, asked Harriet why she didn't like him. Harriet was shocked; if anything Ed was her first friend at work. Ed revealed that Harriet's manager had told him very detailed criticisms about her shirking workloads. In addition, he had been told that Harriet didn't like him. It didn't take long to track down the source. Both Ed and Harriet felt relieved that the bond of their friendship had prevented a potential catastrophe between them.

Bob was not so fortunate. He was one of the other engineers that had been discussed. Criticism of any kind went right to his core. If anything, his work approached perfection to avoid criticism. When Bob was told by another engineer about negative rumors which were circulating about him, Bob felt stabbed in the heart. Unable to control himself, he asked many people in his division if they knew the source of the rumor about his alleged poor work performance. There was no one willing to reveal the obvious source, in part because he looked upset.

Bob's search for the besmircher of his character was fruitless, but he persisted to the point of demanding an immediate work evaluation from his own boss. His boss was confused, for Bob had been a model employee. But now Bob was upset, distracted, and not functioning well at work. He persisted in pleading for a denunciation of rumors which his boss had never heard. He almost lost his job as a result of the tense demands. The rumor spreader eventually was fired, but not before wreaking an immense amount of interpersonal conflict.

ANALYSIS
REVEALING PERSONAL
FEELINGS IS RISKY

Babbling Brook reveals definite weaknesses in the speaker. Unfortunately, that weakness also infects everyone who actively listens. The danger for the listener is either being accused later on of helping aim and fire the torpedos or going down in the babbler's own sinking ship. The babbler's weaknesses are insecurity, jealousy and envy, uncontrollable resentment and anger, and impulsivity. In this case it is possible to answer the philosophical question: does a babbling brook make noise if there is no one there to hear it? The answer is no.

COPING
WITH THE INCLINATION
TO GOSSIP

■ Avoid partaking in private hearings of criticisms of others.

■ Avoid being a babbler, no matter how right or angry you are.

■ Be sure to know the difference between babbling and valid, substantive criticism of others' work. Work-related criticisms should be in formal evaluation reports, as well as direct communications to you about your own work from those in authority to make the evaluation. Any report, formal or otherwise, which includes assessments of a personality weakness or character flaws has evidence of babbling in it. Be wary of participation.

■ A brook that babbles to you about someone else will babble to someone else about you.

HOT FLASHES

Todd spent fifteen years as a design engineer in the steel plant. Initially he was the person with all the new ideas. As time wore on he fell behind in his creativity and slipped into the role of refining established equipment. Two other designers, ten years his junior, had recently been pushing for total design modification of the equipment. Todd's after dinner alcohol consumption had recently increased to the point where it was becoming difficult for him to get to work on time in the morning. What made it so difficult for Todd was realizing the technology the two designers were suggesting was too advanced for him. He had no idea what they were talking about.

It wasn't long before Todd was coming in late for work and complaining bitterly about the two younger engineers. Before the company had any idea that Todd had outdated himself, it reluctantly fired him for alcohol and personality problems.

ANALYSIS

THE PERSONAL EXPRESSION OF AGING

CAN SET DIFFERENT TERMINATION TRAPS

Hot Flashes is one of the few Set-Ups that is accomplished without much help from the institution. The trap is time and change mixed with an unwillingness to view work (and maybe life) as a constant search for growth and development. In some cases Hot Flashes can occur simply because technology marches forward too quickly in a highly competitive atmosphere. Jobs with these risks are not for those with small hormone reserves. In Todd's case he unilaterally let his skills go, spoke negatively about others, and drank—all of which undermined his job.

Another variation of Hot Flashes is called Wrinkles. This can occur to women who have bought into sexist stereotypes (and to some who haven't). Usually the woman suffering from Wrinkles has taken a job for which she had no skills other than her potential and her physical appearance. Time passes, and the potential is never adequately realized. Soon unwrinkled flesh begins knocking on the personnel door. Or, maybe, the boss is no longer "lusting in his heart" for the unrealized lady. The first sign of Wrinkles is seen in two places simultaneously: the mirror at home and the lack of skills at work.

One other variation of this problem has to do with being discriminated against solely on the basis of your age. This is a much discussed topic of late and also a dynamic to be on your guard against. Coping with Wrinkles is a major dilemma for anyone forced out of work solely for reasons of age.

COPING

WITH GROWING OLDER AND ALLOWING
YOURSELF TO BECOME DESKILLED

■ Watch out if you find yourself resenting younger employees; this can be an early reversible signal. If someone brings in new ideas about how your job should be performed, and your response is anger and resentment, then at least recognize you have set your own Termination Trap.

■ Don't conclude that the threat is coming from those people with their new ideas. The threat comes from inside you and has very much to do with your attitudes, capacity for change, and stamina.

■ Keep clear in your head that it's your heart that is threatened. If you lose the ability to analyze what your deficiencies are and change them, the trap will get closer.

■ Incorporate new ideas into your framework and test them out. Reject the ones that don't pass your test.

■ Don't allow the Hot Flashes to distract you. Avoid using alcohol and drugs to quiet your hurt and anger.

■ Don't take a job for which you are not skilled.

■ If you suspect that your age is the only issue, do not act alone in dealing with the problem. Consider hiring an attorney and asking for objective help. Your attorney will be able to guide you through the process of collecting the appropriate information to determine if age discrimination is an issue.

INDIRECT SET-UPS

What makes a Set-Up indirect is the way the behavior flows toward the employee. Direct Set-Ups are aimed straight at the individual employee, the indirect ones flow through the organization and influence everyone equally. The flow begins with the administrative style of the leadership.

The Set-Up comes from the process of the events, not their content. The process is determined by the message, or theme, underlying a series of actions that occur at work. For example, consider the following events: your boss walks by you and looks down, rather than at you; or, you are no longer receiving memos from two important sources; or, your parking place was taken away from you by formal administrative decree; or your boss's secretary forgets to invite you to the company picnic. Each event is behaviorally unique. If you were to confront each person behaving this way toward you, you would probably discover there is a rational explanation which diminishes the event's significance (i.e., your boss was upset with someone else when he looked down, the memos you aren't getting are "no big deal," it's only a little matter to lose your free parking, and the secretary just made a mistake). But the process of each event, the underlying theme, is that you are being rejected. If you can recognize what the underlying message is, then you can control your inclination to react purely with feelings. It is then possible for you to begin rationally solving any problems that might exist.

Most Indirect Set-Ups have similar underlying mechanisms: there is something destructive about the administrative style which prods employees into behavior that invites them to become scapegoats. The term "administrative style" describes the sum of all behaviors that come from management, underlying all decision making. The administrative style of a company is the way it goes about making decisions and carrying those decisions out. A positive administrative style in one company could be experienced as negative in another. If in the heat of combat, a platoon leader held a meeting to obtain consensus on how to handle the problem of the present firefight, too many people could get killed. At that moment someone has to be in charge with very directive comments that will be obeyed. Yet, in other situations, that same leader might meet with his platoon in order to determine the best way to get from one place to another. During this meeting the administrative goals might be consensus, cooperation, and even open disagreement.

Most employees who survive in organizations understand that there are many forces which serve to thwart and frustrate everyone's capabilities. These traps make everyone uncomfortable. Each trap has the capacity to result in job termination, but early detection provides the opportunity to position yourself positively.

TELEPATHY

Two weeks of preparation left Frances feeling very confident about her fall coat designs. She was one of thirty designers working for Mr. Morris's upcoming show. Her peers were dynamic, bright, and energetic. The philosophy of the company was appealing; everyone received individual credit for their designs. Mr. Morris took public pride in his ability to get along with his employees. He liked his own sensitivity and frequently complimented himself for not throwing tantrums the way his competitors did. Outwardly he seemed very subdued and controlled. On top of it all, Mr. Morris seemed to enjoy running the sweatshop end of things. He spent most of his time with the tailors, watching the process of translating the design into cloth. Frances hated this part of the process; she liked to design.

During the last design meeting with Mr. Morris, Frances was openly pleased with her own designs. He seemed to listen attentively. She felt confident he'd take over and handle the manufacturing. During the making of the garments, he was careful to call

her in to ask her specific questions about each coat. Each time he would let her know that he felt he understood the rest of each design.

A few days before the designs were to go public Frances was shocked to discover each of her coats had been changed significantly. The labels had her name right underneath Mr. Morris's; they were her coats, they just didn't look right. Panic-stricken, she went to a few of the other designers. They, too, were upset; the same had happened to them. They were not surprised however. One friend told her it always happened that way.

Frances stormed into her boss's office loudly demanding an explanation. Mr. Morris's voice became softer as the red color rose in his face. Slowly and carefully he lectured to her about his ability to understand exactly what his designers mean by their designs. He was emphatic that the coats labeled with her name next to his were her coats; the *true* expressions of her design ideas as *he* understood them. He reminded her of his ability to understand people. He felt confident that the coats with her name on them represented her true wishes. He also reminded her that his design house took pride in the absence of tantrums and selfish displays of feeling. Frances felt her anger was suffocating her. No one had told her she was working for a psychic who did whatever he wanted because he could read minds with his understanding. Worst of all, she was so upset that she couldn't figure out if his changes made her coats better or worse. All she could feel was anger and hurt.

Two weeks later her coats were removed from the racks. The buyers had placed too few orders to make the manufacturing of them feasible. By now Frances was without an appetite, totally sleepless, tense, and constantly ruminating. To top off everything, Mr. Morris called her into his office to tell her she was fired. He was openly disappointed in her coat designs; they were a complete failure. He also intimated something about her huge rage reaction a few weeks before.

ANALYSIS
THE USE OF POWER
TO KEEP CONTROL

Telepathy represents an administrative style that exerts power over everyone equally. It is Frances's response that got her fired. By responding the way she did she stepped into the Termination Trap. She bought into the Set-Up and offered herself up as the sacrificial lamb. Her problem was a combination of her employer giving out a wrong job definition and her inaccurate perception of what her job was.

With Indirect Set-Ups it is not unusual for the employees to know what is going on and also have very clear ideas of what needs to be done to make things better. Yet, many people sense that to do anything to create changes also creates serious job risks. Often people wait for someone like Frances to blow it and do something. With Indirect Set-Ups, after someone like Frances does her thing and loses her job, things often change for the better. So there are also pressures in the work group for the scapegoating of individuals.

The manager, or institution, that employs Telepathy is unable to feel creative enough to come up with his or her own ideas, yet lacks the confidence to let go and allow others to express their creativity. Bosses who use Telepathy to insert their own ideas into work situations are generally fearful of confrontation and disagreement. Most of their employees feel controlled and manipulated in all aspects of their work.

COPING
WITH HAVING YOUR MIND READ
AND YOUR INTENTIONS THWARTED

■ One thing that Telepathy emphasizes is the importance of knowing the management style and employer before the job is taken. This is often a luxury in difficult economic times, so there are other approaches. It is still important to read your job description closely. Try to meet with present and past employees to inquire about management's style.

■ Knowing that Telepathy can happen is half the battle, if you end up caught in this situation. The major problem with Telepathy is not that someone thinks that he or she can read your mind, it is that they can use that pseudo-knowledge against you.

■ Consider asking the psychic for feedback during the course of each discussion. Do not accept general statements of support; ask for the specifics. Be willing to draw out the criticisms. If the psychic is willing to reveal his or her own ideas, be absolutely certain not to be defensive (even though you may feel it). If your project is going to be changed anyway, isn't it better for it to be done out in the open and not by Telepathy?

GUILLOTINE
INTENTIONALLY SETTING
A TERMINATION TRAP
BY SEARCHING FOR
A SCAPEGOAT

The scenario is quite familiar. A mistake is made that is public and serious enough that retribution is necessary in order to take the pressure off. Guillotine occurs most often in politically sensitive work situations. A mistake is made as a result of a series of multi-level decisions; and many people carry the responsibility for the error. In politics, as well as most corporations, there is some form of accountability. There is also the inclination on most people's part to get quick closure, or ending, to the problem. The most difficult and time-consuming way to gain closure is to study the problem and discover the pathways to the error. This approach is the most

helpful and honest way to prevent future problems. In many situations, however, time does not allow for study. What is needed in highly competitive, heavily politicized, situations are "results." Often the immediate result that is most cost effective when it comes to time, personnel, and money, is finding one person to blame for the problem. This person can be nominated and elected by quiet consensus. This person can be recruited and invested (with enough authority so others will believe he or she did do it all). This person could also be created (against his or her will) and guillotined. It is not unusual for members of a group who work in a highly visible, sensitive arena to agree to manage according to the Guillotine principle: When a mistake is made, someone who is expendable is offered up as the sacrificial wrongdoer. The purpose of this sacrifice is to preserve the group's existence in the face of outside criticism. This leaves employees constantly aware that a trap has been set.

It is difficult to accept how dark the forces can be in group situations. For many people, group survival comes as a result of their being the most fit to survive. These people cloak their asocial nature beneath veneers thicker than their own self-awareness. Many people want power and authority to do important things, but few people are willing to accept the consequences for making mistakes. People who like and use power insure their positions of influence by having others positioned to accept the criticisms and carry the blame. This intentional scapegoating is often explained away by employing a shifting morality: "It's for the good of the company (or Party)," "We need to do this so the group can continue to do its important work," or "It's really that person's fault, and not mine, because. . . ."

Keep your skills of knowing yourself and the group you belong to sharply honed. The prevention of being scapegoated is an art. There are too few prescriptions for this complex phenomenon. Most of what is contained in this book is directly or indirectly oriented toward dealing with being scapegoated.

You have to know when the Termination Trap of being scapegoated has sprung and caught you. One of the hardest things to convince someone of is how futile it is to undo being scapegoated. People who have been scapegoated often worsen their plight by twisting around after the guillotine has lopped off their professional credibility. Writhing around publicly, after being scapegoated, results only in a loss of personal credibility and dignity. Most people sense that in order to be scapegoated a person has to willingly participate in some way or other.

Once you have been publicly scapegoated the best way to cope is to either accept the fact or hire a lawyer and fight your way back in before it is too late.

APRIL FOOLS

Ina was in the first year of her job as the fifth-floor manager of a large department store: all of household furnishings and children's clothing. A day didn't go by without her considering major decisions in product purchasing, marketing and sales, advertising, and floor displays. Resources were allocated during weekly meetings of the floor managers and the general manager. First the groups would review the previous week's cash flow. Ina had three separate cost centers to watch over. During the meetings each manager would discuss short-term (one to four weeks) and long-range (one to six months) planning for their floors.

Ina had new ideas for blending the summer's end buying surge right into the Christmas rush. She had spent days working out the connections between advertising, store displays, and inventory purchases to carry out this marketing strategy. While waiting for the

budget allocations, she was aware how favorable the store manager was toward her ideas. He openly supported her entire plan. On the blackboard in front of everyone were her figures for inventory, personnel, advertising, and displays. He had written them down as he listened to her. He told her to go with it.

Three months later she still had not received a memo documenting the meeting's decisions. She continued to commit her prior budget allocation, assuming the additional monies would come. The only thing that arrived was a slowly progressive depression and anxiety that weighed her down.

One day at lunch two other floor managers listened to Ina's frustration and tentatively shared with her that what had happened was usual. They had learned to present only those ideas that fit within the prior year's budget. Any money allocated beyond that was considered icing on the cake. They had never known an original idea to be followed and accomplished unless the person carried it off without telling management. The rule was not to ask for anything, nor believe you'd get it if promised.

Ina was relieved when she discovered there was nothing personal in the rejection. During her psychotherapy she expressed how glad she was that she didn't let go of her anger while at work. "My bosses don't give much and they don't take much either," was her important insight.

ANALYSIS
WITHHOLDING AUTHORITY
TO CONTROL OTHERS

Management by illusion is not unusual. The pressure to appear progressive and innovative far exceeds the usual time frame for people to want to make changes. It is unusual, in the absence of catastrophies, for any stable, profitable business to accept new ideas quickly. Consequently many promises are made to support the illusion of change, while support is much slower, if ever, to come.

This is a classically incomplete transaction: just at the point where one person feels that both people understand one another, he or she discovers the agreement never existed. The employee who doesn't understand those regressive forces in institutional life runs the risk of expressing the frustration and anger inappropriately. This comes across like the anger of someone not understanding a harmless April Fools joke, or a small child's anger at not getting what he wants. The response from management is usually one of shocked paternalism: "Yes, we did say we would give that to you, but don't you understand that things change?" The things that change are never made clear. The indefiniteness of these kinds of explanations implies there are deficiencies in the employee, rather then an unkept promise on the part of administration. This only serves to further the humiliation.

COPING

WITH FORCES AT WORK THAT BLOCK
YOUR PROFESSIONAL GROWTH

■ Have a clear idea before accepting a job how management handles innovation. Ask to see the long-term plans. It is also important to look at the long-range plans from five and ten years previous. Check the company's present position against those past long-range plans to see just how much was attained. Check with those who are interviewing you to find out who creates future goals. Also meet with those who are identified as carrying through with the plans. Try to get a sense of these people's work styles and approaches. The idea here is to feel confident interviewing those people who are interviewing you. In a progressive company, your straightforward, task-oriented questions will seem informed, interested, and enlightened.

■ Be sure to allow others to test the waters of change and watch carefully what happens (unless you have your own clear sense of how management allocates its resources).

■ Avoid taking it inside and personalizing it. If you do, management will then consider you naive, weak, or unable to fend for yourself. The danger in this interaction is that when April Fools is played out at work, the instigator never considers it a serious problem. You can make people nervous if you hold them as accountable as they should be. People who make other people uncomfortable can lose their jobs.

■ Consider taking notes at meetings and reading them back "just for clarification." These notes can serve as external consciences to those who might want to back out of an agreement. If feasible, implement changes in small steps, keeping your larger goals to yourself. This will seem less threatening to other levels of management and avoid taxing budgetary resources.

■ Remember to stay in close constant contact with the person who made the promise for resources. Do this through weekly memos which outline your activities. As postscripts ask for any possible changes in the plans. This may not get around your not getting what was promised, but it certainly will help you avoid a delayed April Fools!

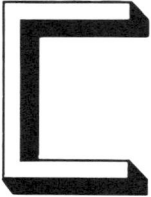

THE FBI
WITHHOLDING
INFORMATION
IS DESTRUCTIVE

If your boss uses unidentified authority above him in the organization to criticize your work, and you find yourself frustrated and annoyed at being unable to acquire specific reasons for these criticisms, there is a problem. If you get memos specifically addressed to you, your section, or division, which outline criticisms, but it isn't clear who the "we," "us," or "they" are who are doing the criticizing, you've got even bigger problems. Clearly there is mystery here, and subterfuge.

You do not really know if you are under surveillance by someone outside your general sphere of influence (and now that person has put the screws to your boss), or if the criticisms are from your boss in disguise. This kind of behavior is seen in organizations which have no clear lines of authority. It could be that someone else's job is in dire jeopardy and you are being used as a pawn to establish a paper trail leading to some other culprit. There is a remote possibility, if the criticisms are valid, that they have risen from outside the company (a client may have complained about you), and the institution has no formal way of handling these complaints. In this situation the "we" or "they" is left open so no one has to substantiate the criticisms.

The Termination Trap has been set, no matter what the reason, because the organization has offered criticisms without identifying the source(s). It is only appropriate to consider your job is in jeopardy.

There is the possibility your boss is doing this directly to you and no one else. In this case the transaction should be taken personally and is called a "J. Edgar Hoover." The analysis is the same.

To deal with this criticism, admit whatever validity the criticisms may have, no matter what the source. Do this first, and without excuses or "buts." You want to establish credibility and resilience. You also want to separate the valid criticisms from the invalid ones. Try to separate both kinds of criticisms from the secret interaction of FBI.

Clarify distortions or inaccuracies next. Identify those criticisms which you are certain are wrong, or probable misperceptions, in a memo to your boss, as well as in conversations with him or her.

Repeat the valid criticisms, state you did hear them, and you will work on them straightaway. If the criticism comes verbally, write it down while it is being said to you. Read it back to the person conveying it. When you get to indefinite pronouns or diffuse accusations stop and ask if you heard that correctly. If the person says yes then you should ask gently for specifics. Who said it, when, where? If there is a reluctance to go further, then carefully point out that the only documentation of the criticism is what you have written down right there. Ask your boss to write a memo documenting what was said to you. If your boss won't, the trap tightens.

Review your notes, state you will type them up as a memo of record and get a copy to your boss. If your boss instructs you not to, that everything is off the record for "your own good," then you should see the trap clearly, and feel it closing in around you. You might point out that if the criticisms are for your own good, it is hard to feel the positive parts of it. It feels more like people are upset with your work performance, and they aren't willing to identify themselves.

Calmly state that the situation feels very serious to you, and you will work hard on the criticisms. Go back to the issues for which you are being criticized and deal with each openly and honestly. Repeat the process of flushing out the source of your discomfort. Your only hope is to find out who to talk with about this. If the criticism comes by memo, then go to the writer of the memo and return to discussing openly and honestly the substance of the allegations.

You are under attack. Either this is an Indirect Set-Up with you (and others) at risk to jeopardize your job by reacting without understanding, or this is a Push-Out (see later).

MANAGERS CAN CONTAMINATE
THE ATMOSPHERE

There are Indirect Set-Ups where managerial attitudes and feelings end up contaminating the work environment. The net result is an increase in work tension and job dissatisfaction which often renders the unsuspecting vulnerable to putting their jobs on the line.

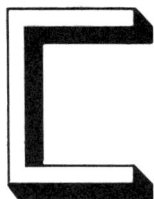

MOUNT ST. HELENS
PERSONAL FEELINGS ARE INFECTIOUS

Do things get done at work only when there is a crisis concerning unrealistic deadlines? Does disorganization filter down from your boss in the form of panicky messages to get something done "by yesterday"? Are there frequent last minute, time-consuming changes which force you into high states of tension and irritability? Do you find yourself knowing that you have to add an extra week onto every job assignment because something always happens near the end to slow you down?

What we are looking at is a managerial style with underlying mechanisms which are as varied as each personality involved. One individual can throw a whole company into this kind of chaos. Sometimes the manager is a meticulous perfectionist who keeps remembering another detail that has to be attended to. With this person there is always the potential for another change in plans, another crisis, because something that no one knew about didn't get done. Sometimes almost everyone seems to be functioning in a Mount St. Helens mode. Many creative businesses, such as the recording and tape industries, live theater, and professional athletics, have regular crises as part of the ambience and quality control.

Examine your own work style first. Is this work style of deadline pressures a problem for you now because you never did like the excitement of volcanos, or have you gotten tired and frustrated with your old style of working? Try to organize more planning sessions where discussions of this problem can begin. Avoid blaming any one person for the "eruptions." Remember this can be an organizational problem, not a personal one. Keep clear in your mind the sources of the crises. Often the causes can come from totally outside your company (unpredictably delayed deliveries, raw material cut-offs, etc.). Seek general solutions that do not serve to scapegoat people or the task, but rather address whatever outside issues exist. Examine how assignments that eventually turn into eruptions are initially given. Consider what alternatives are available to you to control your own productivity schedules without having to be caught in the explosion, or the trap of reacting openly to it. Often the assignment is not clear, or your boss allows too many accommodating compromises, but at the last minute (as usual) wants it "his way."

IN-GROUPS ARE POTENTIAL
TERMINATION TRAPS

In-groups are a phenomenon in many situations, including work. The bonds within these subgroups are very powerful. Contemporary examples of in-groups are the Saudi Family in Saudi Arabia, the Kennedy family and friends in the J.F.K. White House, the socially powerful royal houses in Europe, as well as the socially powerful sorority and fraternity houses on American college campuses.

Not belonging to a group at work can be a neutral or an ominous sign. If the in-group controls your productivity, or if you react emotionally to your nonmembership (even if the in-group is functioning poorly), there is the potential for falling into a trap. Certainly an in-group that huddles together to perpetuate and condone incompetence is a neutral force in your work-life providing it doesn't get in your way.

Understanding in-group phenomena offers you the chance to cope effectively with the dynamics that get in the way of effective job performance.

Notice that in-group members invariably develop common beliefs and norms which get in the way of critical thinking and reality testing. There will be profound pressures on you to adopt the same thinking style. There are in-group words that have a simplicity and elegance to them which can be contagious. These words develop a breadth and "truth" about them that is difficult to contest: "New Frontier," "New Deal," "Great Society." These political words mobilized many people to move politically and expeditiously. They also reflect the similarities of thought that pressured people into consensus opinions. Without the vocabulary you are an outsider who will find it difficult to make decisions.

Belonging to any in-group can swell your happiness and confidence to the point of minimizing the possibilities for risks and dangers. Outsiders appear pessimistic to insiders. If you are on the outside, you must expect that your more objective or cautious views will be discounted. If your job description encompasses some of the in-group's activities, there is reason for concern. Others may end up controlling what you are responsible for by manipulating the informal networks of power in the organization.

In-group members are rendered less competent as individuals. They cannot express individual personal doubts about controversial projects, goals, or planning. Members of in-groups are also at constant risk for losing their jobs. Those on the inside may not be processing information clearly enough to make appropriate decisions. How closely the in-group members sit with the power and authority in the institution must be examined.

In-group forces impose on the insiders and outsiders a constant illusion of consensus. Decisions become more contaminated by the distortions which come from the common beliefs, ideas, language, and perception of nonmembers' animosities. In-group members see nonmembers as threatening nonbelievers, which squeezes the in-group members even closer together. This makes it even more difficult for the in-group members to think objectively.

It does not take long for in-groups to develop internal policing functions. Members with deviant opinions find their ideas suppressed by calls to allegiance to the cause or group. This is just further evidence of the lack of critical thinking and action.

If the leadership of the in-group is charismatic, it serves to solidify all of the above people into one cohesive force. Charismatic leaders speak to very primitive forces within groups. There is something about the leader which people wish to identify with or aspire toward. The values that the leader holds will have a profound impact on the directions that the in-group takes. Whether you are on the inside or the outside of the group, there is great peril here. Group leadership is a narrow tightrope between glory and total failure. How you relate to the leader of the group is a sensitive issue for every other member. The leader symbolizes the entire group's existence. The position that you have in relation to the group is expressed through your interaction with leadership. This is certainly true in any work group, but it is magnified greatly in in-groups.

The last factor to analyze is the group's power base. An in-group can be powerful enough to prevent you from exercising your expertise without fearing for your job. Understanding the real tension between your formal position in the company, the informal power base of in-groups, and the tasks that need to be accomplished is crucial to you. It is this level of understanding which allows you some job security.

To work successfully with an in-group, regardless of being inside or outside the group, use whatever available insight and understanding you have to study what happens. In-groups comprise a series of ongoing, rapidly changing power bases. Knowing this and keeping your finger on the pulse of these changes, offers you the opportunity to avoid being scapegoated. Have confidants whose objectivity you trust close by. They should serve as a constant resource to help you monitor the rapidly shifting changes you will have to cope with. Keep your own moral and ethical beliefs as close to you as possible. You can't help but notice how viciously those beliefs of yours that disagree with the group will be attacked.

Remember that a Set-Up is a chance to get fired, maintain the status quo, or learn and climb upward. The intent of a Set-Up is not to fire you. To get fired you must participate in the process. You can avoid it!

CHAPTER

5

GIVING YOURSELF
A CHANCE
PERSONAL STRESSES YOU
CAN MANAGE NOW

I f Termination Traps are a usual part of work, then so is the stress associated with them. If the trap does begin to close on your job, and work turns sour, it is important to handle your stress well enough to enable you to maneuver out of the problem.

RED FLAGS OF STRESS

Very often the first clue to work-related stress comes from your own body, behaviors, and feelings. Recognizing these symptoms may be the first step towards acknowledging how far the difficulties at work have infiltrated into your personal life. Knowing what is going on will give you some sense of control; and it is important to feel in control of some aspects of your life when work is in turmoil. Knowing that the symptoms and signs are part of a stress reaction points you in the direction of alleviating the stress. Less stress will leave you better able to cope with the work environment.

The following chart lists how your body, your actions, and your thoughts and feelings can send clear messages of being trapped at work.

THE THREE SIGNALS OF STRESS

BODY SIGNALS	BEHAVIORAL SIGNALS	FEELING SIGNALS
Ulcers	Compulsive eating	Food cravings
Diarrhea	Rage reactions	Loss of appetite
Indigestion	Inability to relax	Poor concentration
Constipation	or slow down	Prolonged anxiety
Nausea or vomiting	Biting or tearing	or tension
Stomach cramps	fingernails	Fatigue
Dry mouth and throat	Impulsive purchases	Indecisiveness
Migraine headaches	Decreased sexuality	Racing thoughts
Tension headaches	Curtailing of hobbies	Panicky feelings
Early awakening	Increased alcohol use	Poor frustration
Trouble falling	Increased drug use	tolerance
asleep	Increased mistakes	Apathy
Shortness of breath	at work and home	Boredom
Grinding teeth	Increased minor	Feeling that things
Allergies	accidents	always go wrong
Asthma		Feeling trapped
Frequent colds		Depression
Minor infections		
Heart palpitations		
Change in menses		
Menstrual distress		
Hyperventilation		
Cold hands and feet		
Aching muscles		
Low back pain, hives		

SOME MISTAKEN IDEAS
ABOUT STRESS

Stress Is A Minor Problem; Ignore It. There is a lot of good data to indicate that living with the symptoms and signs of excessive stress can be cumulative and seriously harmful. It is better to work every day to reduce stress before the long-term effects become evident.

If You Feel Fine, There Is No Stress. Many people have the capacity to cover up and hide their signals of stress. Maybe they have learned how to cope with a lot of stress and still function. Yet, high levels of stress contribute to a lowering of our bodies' defenses. Suicide, cirrhosis, lung cancer, accidents, heart disease, and emphysema are all major killers that to a great degree result from poorly managed stress. Working on the early clues of stress, such as a slight elevation in blood pressure, takes diligence and discipline. It may be easier to slow down and relax *after* a heart attack or stroke, but it isn't better for your health.

Everything Is Stressful, So Why Bother. In order to walk a mile, one has to take the first step. The idea that nothing is worth solving because there is too much to do is its own source of stress. People who give in to work stress are the surest victims.

All Stress Is Bad For You. There is always a certain amount of stress (called signal anxiety) which serves to motivate us, prod us onward. Without this healthy and energizing push, much of life would be empty. It is important to remember, however, that yesterday's energizing signal anxiety can be today's overwhelming stress if you have changed. Getting to work on time can be easy when you drive your own car. All that changes with a bulky cast on a broken ankle. We often forget that subtle changes in us can diminish our capacity for handling usual stresses.

THINGS TO DO
TO REDUCE STRESS

Important Little Things You Can Do Now

1. Make a list of all those big things in the world around you that make you feel more ill at ease.

   ■ The news (on TV or in the papers)

   ■ Local or national politics

   ■ Traffic

   ■ Crowding

   ■ Odors or noise

   ■ Violence in your neighborhood

Get the idea? Your list could be longer. Now how many of these can you solve right now? Maybe you could change your way of getting to work to avoid some of the traffic hassles. If it will help reduce the stress on you during your rough time at work, do it. Narrow your focus by shutting out some extraneous stressors. Consider missing the evening TV news and read the newspaper instead—newspapers aren't as visually stimulating and emotionally loaded. Don't be ashamed to use a nighttime blindfold or ear plugs if there is something that has been interrupting your sleep.

2. Make a list of life events apart from work that are stressful. Now this list could be endless to be sure. The following is just a guideline. Be specific with your lists. Don't forget the little things.

   ■ Family problems
   > Marital difficulties
   > Deaths
   > Discipline problems
   > Drug problems
   > Sexual difficulties
   > Illness

   ■ Financial problems

   ■ Personal problems
   > Something you don't like about yourself
   > Anxiety about your skill levels
   > Thoughts that are negative, self-defeating
   > Persistent tensions not related to work
   > Problems with assertiveness

You will need family support during the stress of the job crisis. Sit down with someone you trust and discuss this list. This may be the time to consider meeting with an accountant or a debt counseling service. It may be the time to use company insurance to hire a competent therapist to help you work on these problems. Solving these problems in the middle of a job stress can increase your sense of hope. At the very least develop a plan for working on each of the items in this list; even if the plan is to ignore the problem (as long as that will diminish the stress!). Allowing these nonwork-related problems to persist unattended will increase the wear and tear on you now that work is also stressful.

3. Now stop making lists.

4. Consider getting a physical examination. Consider using part of your lunch time for a daily exercise program and shower. Both are very relaxing.

Little, But Important, Things
To Do At Your Desk
To Help You Relax

■ Be certain your chair is comfortable. If it can't be made comfortable, then change it.

■ Change the intensity of your telephone's ring, if it needs that.

■ Examine and change the lighting at your workplace. The goal is to remove glare or dimness.

■ Come to a decision about how you really feel about your office furniture. If you have never personalized your work space do it now. Bring in pictures of family, or a lamp from home, or something personal.

■ If you have a door to your office, reconsider whether or not to leave it open. How do you feel about it now? If you have no way to be alone at work, find a place somewhere in the building where you can take breathers (as opposed to coffee breaks).

■ Examine your style of dress. Tight shirt collars can cause light-headedness and ringing ears because of decreased blood flow to the brain. Tightly cinched belts and tight-fitting clothes force people to breathe more from their chests than their abdomens. This can cause light-headedness and panic attacks.

■ Establish a regular time for meals, especially lunch. The regulation of blood sugar and the body's biological clock are finely tuned mechanisms that do much better on a schedule. Eating the right foods is critical. Protein, in the form of nuts and fowl, is a good way to smooth out blood sugar variations. Be wary of forcing your body to gain energy from starch. If you notice that each day at a certain time you need caffeine to keep going, then examine your dietary deficiencies. The caffeine could be needed in order to force the adrenal glands to pump out the epinephrine to release the sugar stored in your liver. That epinephrine will also increase your body's stress load. More than three cups (not mugs) of coffee has the serious potential for overstimulating your body. This includes the caffeine in tea and soft drinks, as well as the theobromine stimulant in chocolate.

■ Teach yourself how to breathe properly and how to relax by doing the following exercise.

Breathing Exercises For Relaxation

Do this exercise for five minutes at least three times a day at work. Sit in your (now comfortable) office chair with your hands lying limply in your lap. Slouch down just enough to be able to see your stomach. Keep your focus of attention on your stomach as you breathe. Your stomach should move up with every inhalation and down with each exhalation. Work on making this happen. It is not necessary to take deep or rapid breaths, only to make your abdomen move and to keep your attention focused on doing the exercise. The correct movement of your diaphragm can occur only if you are wearing unrestricted clothing. If you are doing it properly you should be able to put an eraser on your chest and it will not move at all. This means that your diaphragm is pulling in the air and pushing it out.

Too many people believe they should breathe with their chest muscles. It has recently been shown that people who breathe "from the chest" are prone to anxiety and panic attacks because they take in too little oxygen and blow out too much carbon dioxide.

Most people find the experience of the exercise very relaxing. However, the result of learning how to breathe properly is the biggest benefit of all.

Relaxation Exercises

Simple relaxation exercises are very beneficial. Sit back in your chair and concentrate on making your big toe on your right foot relax. You do this by first wiggling it all around (which helps you find it). Then let it go limp while thinking intensely about doing that. When you are satisfied with your success and you are certain that the toe is totally free of energy, then proceed to the other four toes on your right foot. Then to your left great toe (don't rush into this, that will defeat the purpose), and then to the remaining toes. Do this three times a day at your desk. It shouldn't take more than five minutes to do it; but however long, do take the time.

Once you have learned how to make your toes go limp (this should take about five to seven days of slow, unrushed work), then do both feet at the same time. Then progress to relaxing the ankles, calf and foreleg muscles, thighs, abdomen, and so on. Remember you are doing these exercises to cope with stress, so keep it slow. People who have learned this technique of progressive body relaxation can easily institute almost total relaxation within a minute or two. This is very useful for all forms of stress. Remember, start with your toes and do not move upward until the section of the body you are working on is totally relaxed.

Active Imagery and Meditation

Active imagery is a technique which Olympic athletes are now using to better their performance and cancer patients are using to increase their bodies' defenses. This can also be used to cope with stress.

While doing the progressive relaxation it is very helpful to picture scenes that are soothing to you. Pick a scene from a past occurrence in your personal life that has soothed you. Do not choose one you *think* would soothe you. Be very sure it's something you have lived through. If you pick a situation to imagine that was really relaxing to you, you will be calling forth the success of prior experience.

There is another form of active imagery which is far more assertive and distantly resembles that used in Olympic training. With this form of imagery, you conjure up the stress, anger, and frustration that is directly associated with your work experience. Next you imagine the characters who are causing your stress. Lastly, with all of your negative feelings swimming around the images, you resolve the tension by imagining something quite outlandish that relates directly to the workplace. For example, an executive with a lawn supply corporation found herself unusually stressed by her boss's arbitrary and destructive behaviors at work. She was conflicted about work, in that there was a lot about her job which she very much enjoyed. Yet, as time went on, it seemed clear to her that her employment was coming to an end. There was nothing concrete she could put her finger on. The harder she tried at work, the more the tension seemed to mount. Her sense of stress was beginning to constrict her performance at work. It was suggested to her that she consider imagining her boss lying down flat, while she mowed and trimmed him into a perfect lawn. At first she found the thought gruesome and frightening. As time went on it became clear that her stress was far more gruesome than the gentle inner relief she gained from the increasingly humorous imagery.

This can only be recommended for those people who really do know the difference between thoughts and actions, who have no problem controlling destructive impulses, and who are having some trouble resolving their stresses at work because of shifting and conflicting feelings.

Meditation is another technique that can be very helpful. Consider formal training or the less expensive purchase of a book that teaches the skills. Meditation is essentially the same as progressive relaxation and various forms of imagery. Remember that working on eliminating the minor stresses in your life will go a long way to enable you to cope with any major ordeal in the workplace.

6

GOING OUT EASY: RECOGNIZING PUSH-OUTS
THE ONE-WAY TRAPS

D o you have a clear sense that your job is going to be over? You may be the victim of a Push-out. Push-Outs are behaviors directed toward an individual, or a group of people, that are intended to thoroughly convince the person(s) to leave. When it is directed toward one specific individual, the Push-Out is direct; toward many individuals, the Push-Out is indirect. Push-Outs always seem unfair; there are always victims. This is true even if a person is getting fired for legitimate reasons.

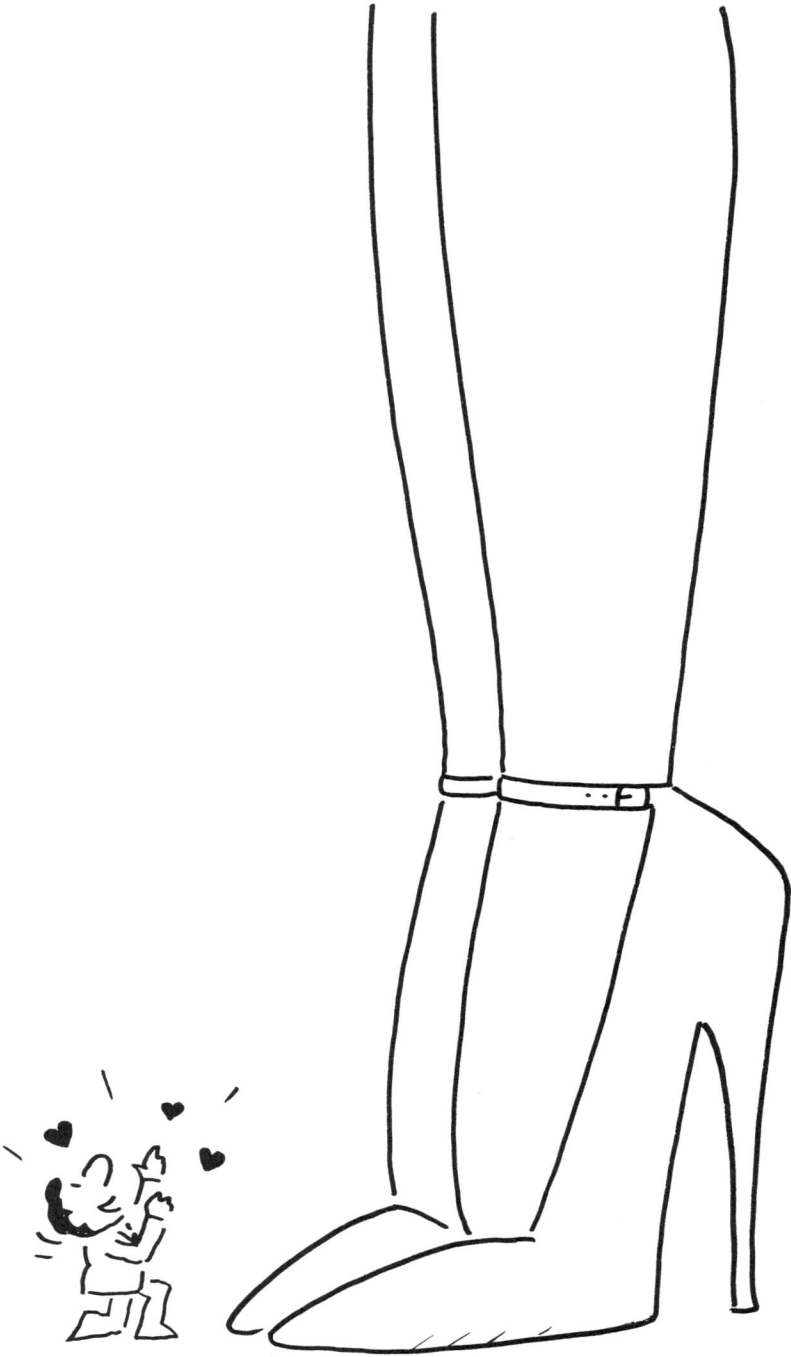

Push-Outs are invariably painful, and it is always very difficult to know what to do to right the situation. The Termination Trap is sprung tighter with Push-Outs than with Set-Ups, and it will seem at first that there is very little that can be done to get free. But, there are always options for coping with the catastrophe of being forced out of your job, even when your thinking is clouded by intense, volatile feelings. Knowing how to channel your anger and resentment into beneficial directions is all part of being able to leave in your own style. Gaining a fair severance, good references, and medical coverage are just a few of the positive benefits that can be yours when you acknowledge your entrapment sooner rather than later.

If Set-Ups are delicate, sophisticated, intricate, and complex, then Push-Outs are crude, hard-lined, and simple. Remember that the directness of Push-Outs will most likely create strong defensiveness on the part of the victim; people can hide from even the bluntest cues when threatened. The following examples illustrate just how powerful and aggressive Push-Outs can be.

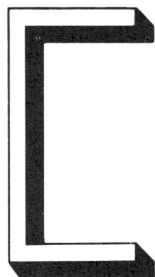

THE IMPOSSIBLE DREAM
(NIGHTMARE?)

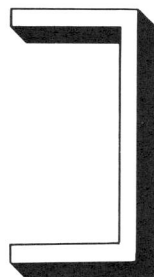

Larry was a manager at a large auto agency. As the head of fleet sales he had been under much pressure in the previous year. First came the poor economy and the precipitous downturn in automobile sales. Second came the inevitable decrease in corporate purchases of fleet auto sales. Third was his boss's increasing tantrums at management meetings. Then, as if that weren't enough, his wife had an unfortunate medical complication which left her partially disabled. There was a lot distracting him, but still he functioned in his usual hard-working, perfectionistic style.

In one managerial meeting, the boss (and owner) announced that all divisions would have to reduce payroll costs by one-third.

Larry protested, stating that most of his time was spent servicing his corporate clients by phone or in person. He felt there was no way he could service old accounts and beat the pavement for new ones if he had to let one of his three (Larry was one of the three) men go. His boss sarcastically reminded him that there was no choice.

Six weeks later, at another meeting, his boss dragged out the computer sheets and began criticizing each manager. When he got to Larry, the issue was decreased fleet sales. Larry brought up the state of the economy, plus the fact that his percentage decrease was no greater than the new or used car sales divisions. He also reminded his boss that servicing old accounts was a fixed time commitment, and with the personnel decrease it was harder to reach out for new corporate accounts. His boss mumbled and moved on to the service manager. After that meeting Larry began to notice that for the first time in his life he did not look forward to going into work. There was no one to discuss this with, for his wife was too ill.

In another four weeks, sitting with the managers, his boss informed Larry that he would have to increase his fleet sales by 30 percent in the next six months. His boss impressed upon him that unless this could be done there was no way for him to vindicate the overhead expense of a separate fleet department. Larry was shocked and felt a slight pain just below his breastbone. He protested that it couldn't be done; the whole economy would have to recover before an increase could occur. His boss countered with a recognition of the bad state of the economy and a pointed comment that Larry would just have to broaden his search for more and larger companies that purchased or leased greater numbers of cars. Larry asked for a return to his usual personnel allotment. His boss laughed and told him to be realistic. Two days later Larry received a memo documenting his boss's expectations.

Larry sweated out the next six months. Never in his life had work been so painful and so frustrating. He knew what his mandate was and he struggled to attain it by working eighty hours per week. The only thing he had to show for it by the end of the six months was a modest increase in fleet leases and sales, chest pains, and severe depression. He was now under a doctor's care. Although he had almost single-handedly increased fleet sales, the results were nowhere near his boss's 30 percent goal.

Almost six months to the day of receiving his mandate his boss walked in and angrily fired him for not "measuring up to expectations." Then followed a half-hour tirade about Larry's incompetence. Larry begged to be laid off. His boss called him naive and asked Larry if he didn't realize why everything had been so carefully spelled out in the memo. There was no way he was going to have Larry's leaving increase his unemployment insurance. Larry was told that he had been given six months to "perform" and he hadn't "hacked it." He was given one hour to clear his desk and "get out."

ANALYSIS

USING POWER TO
ALTER SOMEONE'S CAREER

Many people immediately feel very stressed after being assigned to an impossible job; there is a sudden realization that you've walked right into a trap without any forewarning. Larry was told to do something that was close to impossible to accomplish. Being told to do it is a definite Push-Out; being asked as in a Set-Up, gives one the choice to avoid the failure. This is a fine line, and depends on your boss's style of communication. However, being asked gives you the possibility for waking up from the Impossible Dream and negotiating some release from the trap.

Sometimes, however, being told to do something impossible is *not* an early warning of getting fired. Many government agencies have mandated tasks which are impossible to do. Nonetheless people are hired and paid to work at these tasks. These are rarely considered to be potential traps (unless Jack Anderson finds out about it). These special exceptions can be clarified right from the beginning, if the "victim" is able to understand clearly what, in fact, is happening. As mentioned in a previous chapter, one of the strongest arguments for understanding the more painful dynamics of the workplace is being able to use these understandings during times of stress. Undertaking an impossible task usually results in profound physical and emotional exhaustion. This tiredness leads to all sorts of behaviors that may inevitably result in losing your job, even if the original intent was not to have you go. Being able to think clearly under stress has many "saving" benefits.

COPING
WITH BEING SHOVED INTO
AN IMPOSSIBLE POSITION

■ When presented with an impossible work assignment it is best to confront the person who is assigning the task. It is fair game to say to the person assigning the work that in your estimation the job can't be done. Be prepared to back up that statement with careful documentation. Suggest that it might be better for you to resign with a clean record.

■ If you don't want to state the job can't be done, then at least ask bluntly if your own job is on the line. Point out that the task is not possible and give clear work-oriented data to support this. In this situation you might want two or three days to think about the assignment to pull together your support and reasons for the impossibility of the task. You are also testing whether or not your boss is willing to share the responsibility for failure. This is another place to consider resigning. Weigh factors carefully. It may be possible to hold your job and get out of the trap. Consider the following.

■ Write a memo of record concerning what has transpired up to this point regarding the impossible task. If your boss persists in the assignment, even if he or she assures you that he or she knows the job is impossible but it has to be undertaken to prove to someone else that it can't be done (this does happen), still be certain to write a detailed memo. The memo should clearly establish your exact position. It should also serve to warn the company that by setting you to work on the Impossible Dream it might be wasting valuable resources. Lastly, this memo should serve as a dated document to establish whether or not you were a competent employee. If you get fired, it may be a useful form of financial insurance. The contents of this memo should record:

- All the data which supports your contention that the job is not possible;

- Specific contingencies concerning the task request that could be changed to make it more possible, including everything from personnel and resource allocation to feasibility of accomplishment or marketability of the product or service;

- The help that you asked for to do the job and why it is not available to you;

- Any support from people inside or outside the corporation;

- Appendices of data, technical or business articles, newspaper clippings, or anything that supports your view.

What you are doing is protecting yourself, and the company.

■ Stay alert. Remember that in 1960 it seemed like an Impossible Dream to put a man on the moon within ten years. There is always the possibility that you are being launched on a creative endeavor. However, if that is the case, the signals will be very clear. Nonetheless, if it doesn't work out your job may still be on the line.

■ Some people are assigned many Impossible Dreams and are allowed to stay in favor as long as they are willing to earnestly attempt the tasks. This is a case where the doing is more important than the results. This happens very often in human service work (social work, medicine, physical therapy, etc.). It is very important to realize that if you speak openly about the impossibility in this situation you may seriously jeopardize your job. But remember that it is demoralizing and exhausting to repeatedly attempt to do the impossible. You might be unable to escape the feelings of failure even if no one else cares. In situations like this it is important for the management to figure out ways to nourish and support its employees or for the employees to devise formal or informal support mechanisms and/or groups.

PUSHED OUT BY
THE POWERFUL

Sometimes the person doing a direct Push-Out uses raw power obtained through formal bureaucratic channels, with the support of the organization behind him or her. When attacked in this manner, you will feel the weight of the entire institution pushing on you. It is important to keep thinking clearly.

VIETNAM

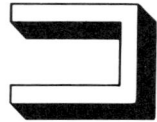

Karen had always been outspoken. At times it got in her way. She was aggressive, but one needed that in order to survive the high pressure of selling insurance. Competing with the men in her office was very difficult. What turned a tolerable job into a painful one was her three-million-dollar year. The men in the office became more openly hostile, and their anti-women jokes more open.

The central office sent a new regional director. He was mildly seductive with all the women in the office. Karen held firm to her idea that her personal life was totally separate from work. She liked and respected him, but found his mild sexual advances annoying. One day he was openly disturbed by her tactful rejections. "You're too much work," he hissed at her. The next day all seemed fine.

A couple of months later the manager announced that he wanted to expand the types of coverage the office offered by taking on policies offered by another company. He told the people in the office that the first problem to be solved was convincing the home office to allow this to take place. He elected Karen to go to the home office and discuss it. He needed to stay with the branch office to work out a new sales program, and he felt she had the push and drive to argue his case effectively. She remembered how vehemently opposed the home office had been to the same idea just two years before. Karen told him that the company he was trying to link up with had been in great disfavor and, in fact, still owed their company some money.

The manager was adamant, and then took a vote to determine who supported his idea. Everyone but Karen voted in favor. The tone of this meeting was particularly gleeful. The part of her that wanted recognition and to do a good job told her to go. All other parts were reluctant, even apprehensive, about the futility of the task. She spent time with her manager discussing his goals and familiarizing herself with their division's activities.

The week before she left she felt anxious and tense. This was not relieved when her boss notified her that she was going to New York with a promotion. He told her she should have enough authority to be listened to. Somehow this only made her feel worse. She was convinced that the whole task was futile. She went, and argued her boss's position aggressively. The battle was intoxicating for her, she was good at it. Halfway through, it even began to feel like her project as she got swept into succeeding.

Two weeks later her boss walked in and suggested that things weren't going too well with her. He told her he was being pressured by the central office to let her go. It seemed they felt her presentation was too aggressive and her style was not representative of the company's image for its employees. She was shocked and angry. Something told her she had been had. It took her a while to put the whole picture together.

ANALYSIS
THE POWER TO MAKE SOMEONE
ELSE FIGHT A LOSING BATTLE

This vignette illustrates just how complex all transactions are. In Vietnam there is: a) the successful woman competing with threatened men; b) the seduction gone awry; c) the dynamics of the sacrificial lamb, or scapegoat; d) the impossible task; e) the double bind—not being able to get ahead without being aggressive, but finding yourself unacceptable if you are; and (f) being sent to fight someone else's battle. All of these occur in the example with Karen.

Vietnam is a prime example of going off to fight someone else's losing battle. This is not a mere Set-Up. Even if you win, you stand a good chance of incurring animosity or jealousy. You have exposed their weakness. Everybody loses in a fight, and it's difficult to win a battle that belongs to someone else.

Certainly sending someone off to do battle is an obvious way to get rid of them. There are few exceptions to the admonition that it is best to avoid picking up and fighting for a cause that is not your own. Besides, you have to wonder what makes the adversary so dangerous that your boss is unwilling to go and do his or her own fighting.

COPING
WITH WAR
AT WORK

■ Ask for a private meeting with your boss. Take notes.

■ Begin by asking for your boss's reasons for sending you into Vietnam. Of course, you've heard the reasons, but you want to appear nonconfrontational at first. It is wise to begin a potentially tense discussion on a familiar subject.

■ Next review just how your boss feels the battle can be won, no matter who fights it. Make it clear to everyone that the battle is not yours. The key to dealing with this situation is not taking on the battle as yours.

■ Then review what special expertise you have to fight this battle. If by now you are convinced the request is fair, then the feeling of entrapment should have disappeared along with your feeling tense (listen with your head and your heart). Go buy a suit of armor and don't be so worried.

■ If you still feel your job is on the line, then bring up your job status by first asking your boss to review with you any problems he or she is having with your work performance or personality. From there the discussion should logically expand into specific areas of your work. This is a risky suggestion because it lets on that you know that the boss considers you expendable. It is best used only if you feel that it is inevitable that you are going to lose your job if you go off and fight the battle.

■ This is one of those few times where it may be fair to "get sick" and be unable to go. This is another risky suggestion. You may be only delaying the inevitable as far as your own job is concerned, the boss could get you for being disloyal, and you have to live with your own feelings of bowing out of the stress. On the other hand, this can be a shrewd move if you are certain that the war will blow over when someone else realizes your boss made the mistake in asking anyone to do the fighting.

■ Refuse to go and insist on discussing why you have been chosen. This is a very confrontative decision and not without its own perils. There may be little difference between this and suffering through the losing battle that you don't believe in and then returning to suffer through getting fired. On the other hand, there may be a big difference, too. You'll have to feel this one out.

■ Help find someone else to go, providing they are more willing or able to do so. There are moral dilemmas here, but the search could give you some time to sort out your job status.

■ If you decide to take on the challenge of the project, then suggest that someone else go with you. The reason is to balance your area of expertise. Be sure to select your boss's favorite soldier. Maybe the "suicide mission" will then be canceled, or at least the possibility of firing one of you will have been undermined.

If you have to go alone be sure that you present the idea as someone else's; you have merely been asked by your boss to present the idea. It isn't your idea, and you should make that clear.

BELCH
PUSHED OUT WITH
NO 'EXCUSE ME'

Jerry was a family practitioner working for a large corporation that owned private hospitals. He had obtained his MD at the age of forty-eight after teaching college history for eighteen years in a small midwestern school. He had chosen to work for this company because it helped him to avoid building a practice. The salary was modest, but fair; and the company prided itself in choosing its medical staff so well that it never let anyone go. Now he was in his late fifties and doing quite well, except with his boss. The problem seemed personal to Jerry, only because he refused to admit his trouble coping with the profit motive in medicine. He also did not like taking orders from a "thirty-two-year-old punk."

The corporation was constantly opening new hospitals around the northern hemisphere. Jerry rarely if ever looked at other job postings. His children lived near him, and he and his wife liked their house and the community. One morning his boss walked in to inform him the corporation had decided to transfer Jerry to a small walk-in satellite clinic in a community 60 miles away. Jerry laughed, he thought it was a joke. His boss stormed out, and nothing more was said.

Four days later Jerry received a letter from corporate headquarters outlining his new job. It was filled with the specifics of where, when, and how. There was no mention of salary increase, promotion, or moving allowance. Otherwise it was detailed, clean and cold. It even closed with a "warm" regards and a "best wishes in your exciting new career."

Jerry was shocked. There was no chance for reprieve. His boss made that very clear. Jerry felt too old, too tired, and too uninterested to make the change. That night, in a psychotherapy session he told his psychiatrist, "You know, he (the boss) just belched me right out of the company without an 'excuse me'. And the person with a sour taste in his mouth is me. It doesn't look to anybody like we're having trouble. His damn record is clean. He knows I don't want to leave." Jerry was acutely depressed. He felt trapped, and there seemed to be no choices available to him. He turned over 300 aspirin tablets he had planned to use and voluntarily entered a hospital.

ANALYSIS
USING BUREAUCRATIC POWER
TO PUSH SOMEONE OUT

Belch is about as close to getting fired without the ceremony that one can get. There is the sudden sense of being blown out of the company without the reality of it happening. All the arrows point to the exit, yet the administration may persist in denying that's the case. The clue here is that the pie was not sweetened with advancement or pay increase. There was merely a directive that Jerry was needed somewhere else.

In Jerry's situation, the memo from corporate headquarters meant that administration supported the manager's decision concerning Jerry. Corporate signals like this are definite Push-Outs. The tone of a memo from headquarters tends to depersonalize the transaction. For all Jerry knew, the company actually did need someone to take that position. If this were the case, then Jerry's manager could have used that need to get rid of him without the company ever knowing there was friction.

COPING

WITH THE MISUSE OF
BUREAUCRATIC POWER

■ You can fight it with frank confrontation or formal appeal. It's best to go around your manager fairly quickly. Just how aggressive to be depends on how much you have to lose. There is always the possibility of finding a more sympathetic ear higher up in the corporation.

■ Remember there is always the chance that upper level management forced this relocation in an attempt to get you (and others) to resign. There won't be a lot of sympathy up there if that's the case. Check whether or not anyone else (especially other older employees) anywhere in the company has been forced into moving.

■ Consider getting legal advice. With an immediate boss who doesn't like you *and* a memo from the corporation pushing you out, it is very difficult to know just what happened. Legal advice will also help you view the situation more objectively. Is your boss following someone else's decision to get rid of you, *or* did he or she engineer your transfer (or dismissal) by using the anonymity of the company? It is worthwhile, if you are unwilling to comply with the Push-Out, to consider a legal confrontation concerning your job status. A lawyer will be helpful, so will a presentation of your "case" to much higher levels of administration. Do not go softly. If you go for setting the record straight, be sure to arm yourself with all the pertinent data that solidifies your competence and accomplishments. You might also prepare any case against the person(s) with whom you did not get along. This may be one trap when you must open up the doors to your own aggression. Having a lawyer on your side who understands business and employment law will help you keep a cooly informed head.

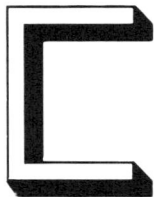

TORPEDO
THE POWER
TO DESTROY

Your boss threatens you with charges that call into question your integrity, competence, and/or character. Simple and direct, from a range of one inch to the distance a memo or phone call can reach, this Torpedo is both a trap that grabs you, and a snare that tightens when you try to get out.

Either, your boss was correct on all counts (and he did a better job then you did); or, your boss was only partially right (and both of you have a lot of work to do to sift things out honestly); or, your boss was mostly mistaken or dishonest (and there's a big fight brewing). It's very hard to miss the point in this situation: you are about to be terminated.

COPING
WITH FOUL PLAY

■ Go straight to your office and pull all papers that belong to you. Copy all documents that protect your job and your reputation. Do this yourself, alone.

■ Take all relevant documents, go home, and cool off; the tension and the sprung trap are too close together to risk an outburst. Find someone you really trust to be your sounding board. This person should have an idea of what is happening independent of your story. You need objectivity.

■ Be careful to avoid drugs and alcohol. It will lower your ability to inhibit those upset angry feelings. It will make it difficult to think clearly.

■ You probably need legal advice. Hire a lawyer right away. You might consider an attorney friend, but if that person cares too much for you personally, then you run the risk of infecting him or her with your upset feelings and reducing his or her clear thinking. Consider hiring the best you can afford. Search around for a lawyer with business experience who has a reputation for clear-thinking firmness. Don't be afraid to choose someone who is known to be a winner. Sometimes these attorneys have controversial public images simply because they are winners.

■ Keep writing memos. Protect your records. Make copies of all sensitive material and put them in a safe place outside the company. Change nothing.

■ Watch out for that horrible sensation of feeling guilty just because you have been accused. This can weaken you at a time when you need to figure out how to climb out of the trap. Remember, your whole career, not just this particular job, may be at stake in Torpedo.

THE ROUNDTABLE AND KGB
USE OF LOYALTY
TO MANIPULATE

Rosemary noted that each time she disagreed with her boss over a matter that related to her work, he questioned her loyalty to the entire company. He suggested that she change her means of product distribution. She disagreed, and then explained how the change would slow her down, be less profitable, and get in the way of other important work. He then won the discussion by telling her that "her attitude prevented her from being a team player." This was not an unusual response from him. He even asked her "why are you always blocking what it is the company needs to do?"

Rosemary repeatedly found that the demands he placed on her seemed to get in her way. She finally tried going to upper level administration. This angered her boss and didn't help change anything. Within a year she was laid off.

ANALYSIS
THE DESTRUCTIVE USE OF
ALLEGIANCE OR TRICKERY

The Round Table has to do with your boss putting allegiance to him or her far ahead of the allegiance to work and the tasks at hand.

KGB is similar, but the attack is more direct: right at your personality. KGB often occurs by way of notes and memos, as opposed to face to face. Somehow, one or all of the following happen: your employee evaluations have been late, unrealistically negative or neutral, and based more on your "bad attitude" than your work performance.

The message in both transactions is clear: you are a member of the group (or party), but in very poor standing. Both The Round Table and KGB are inevitable Push-Outs. No matter what the underlying dynamics are, your job is under attack. With The Round Table you are not free to express your own opinion about your own job without threat of getting fired. Everybody knows when someone questions your loyalty they are examining your membership status in the group. Even if it's only a threat, there is such a strong invitation to react to the assault aggressively or by withdrawing (in fear) that just your reaction, alone, could jeopardize your job.

With KGB someone out there is being very critical of your ''attitude'' and is writing reports about it. This is very dangerous. Those pieces of paper can sit for years in your personnel file. At the very least, they could slow down raises and promotions. It is doubtful they would be used for so benign a reason. When negative reports appear, this is a very ominous sign.

It could be that this all occurs because of your boss's incompetence. Nonetheless, your boss is one step closer to the authority that represents the company. Unless you are an unusually gifted employee you must respond to these direct attacks. These exchanges often occur within in-group settings where there are lots of calls to allegiance, many buzzwords, and an elitist environment.

COPING
WHEN YOU ARE ACCUSED
UNFAIRLY OF LACKING LOYALTY

■ Respond to every accusation with a statement of your loyalty and a clarification of your disagreement. In doing this, separate the substance of the disagreement from your alleged disloyalty to the group or your boss. If necessary write a memo of record and send it to your boss.

■ In KGB you must write a memo to your boss, the personnel department, and maybe your boss's boss outlining your disagreements with the evaluation(s). Be careful with this one, however. If KGB is going on, your memo could get misfiled or lost. Clearly document your work record (loyalty to the company) with all the memos and memos of record you've been keeping. Ask for discussion about your attitude, and be sure to gently confront vague vocabulary and inaccurate statements.

■ In both The Round Table and KGB keep memos of record.

■ As personal as the attack can seem, as important as your defense must be, this is still a good time to consider the possibility that you do have a bad attitude. What is that attitude all about? Is there something about the work you don't like? Or do you have problems with authority? Should you consider a change of jobs? Should you consider professional help to avoid repeating a personal problem at some future job?

A FEW
TENDERIZING
TRAPS

The Invisible Employee. William had this strange feeling that people who passed him in the hall were not looking at him. It was an easy thing to discount at first; besides he felt guilty for feeling suspicious. Then one day his own secretary caught his eye in the hall and quickly looked down. That night he slept very poorly. In the morning he checked his face for pimples. For two more weeks he put up with feeling humilated. Twice he asked two friends in the company if he looked all right. The tension was unbearable for him, but he didn't know where it was coming from. Finally he asked his secretary if she knew of anything. She broke down and cried, telling him that her closest friend who happened to be the secretary to the divisional vice president, had told her a long time ago that William was going to be replaced.

Hospital Ward. On Monday four people came up to Irving at work and asked him if he was sick. It wasn't until his boss also asked him that Irving started to feel a little apprehensive. The facts were that he had felt fine until everyone started asking. That night he asked his wife if he looked well. She thought he was tired and haggard, but otherwise his usual self. He mused with her just how stressed he was feeling at work.

Just two days later, his boss informed him that he wanted the company doctor to look him over. Irving actually felt a little relieved, maybe that would end all the worried glances he had been getting. There was a growing part of him that was beginning to believe he might be sick, given everyone's reactions to him lately.

The company doctor was open and friendly. Irving told him about his mild hypertension, occasional headaches, indigestion, and a past history of ulcers. The doctor did a brief physical exam. The next Monday his boss called him and asked him how he felt. Irving told him the only thing that was upsetting was all the concern about his health. He wondered what the doctor had said. The boss then informed him that the doctor had recommended that Irving take some sick time off from work. Irving exploded. He demanded to see the report. It was there, in black and white, all of his symptoms were exaggerated into a picture of a "sick" man. Topping everything off, his boss told Irving that the explosion was proof of how strung out Irving was.

Irving stormed out feeling "they" were trying to push him out of his job. Irving quickly hired a lawyer to do his communicating for him. Then followed two miserable years for Irving, pretending at work that everything was just fine when all the while his lawyer and the company were involved in heated debate. Irving did manage to keep his job. Two other people at his level were pushed out during this time for "health-related" reasons.

Surgery. Your boss suddenly came at you with a scalpel. This represents an unusual change in his interaction with you. Out of nowhere he became angry with things you said and did that are quite ordinary and usual for you. His behavior was unusual and so was the barrage of criticisms. He also claimed that you "needed" his direct intervention, as if you were incapable of rectifying your own problems.

ANALYSIS
FEELING WELL OR ILL IS
NOT NECESSARILY A PHYSICAL MATTER

These three mechanisms of moving a person out of a company are especially difficult to cope with because they are well hidden. The essential issue is that people really do know there is something wrong with you—you are going to be pushed out. The problem is worsened by their feelings of guilt about knowing something you don't know. They are powerless to relieve their extreme discomfort by telling you directly. Maybe they lack the authority to do so without jeopardizing their own jobs. They also may not have the stomach for telling you. Something has to be done with their discomfort, so they put it on to you. They know, if you knew, that you would feel sick; so they respond to you as if you were sick. What they don't accept is how sick the whole thing makes them feel. Instead of feeling sick, they project it onto you.

Projections are unwanted, unacceptable, or forbidden feelings put onto someone else. Once the feelings are out there, and coming from someone else, the projector can respond more safely to the threatening feelings. For example, in William's case, people saw him as sick rather than acknowledging that what was happening gave them a sick feeling inside. If they acknowledged their own sick feelings then they would have to acknowledge that their jobs, too, were in jeopardy. That was an unacceptable feeling that they projected out onto William, and the projection served to protect them. The problem for William was how confusing and painful the projections were.

COPING
WITH PROJECTIONS

■ Examine Irving's willingness to take a stand on his own behalf. Remember the financial and emotional consequences. Only you can decide when it is right for you to take a stand. It is not possible to cover each specific dilemma that votes "for" or "against" the decision to fight back versus the decision to resign. Fighting back can take the form of a firm short-term stand that signals strong commitment and feelings; or, it can be extended into a long-term legal hassle. It's always hard to know who wins the long legal battles. If you consult an attorney, be certain to review the well-known fact than many juries will vote for the underdog, but the majority of Appeals Courts undo those decisions in favor of the opposing party. Get these specifics from your attorney; then decide your course.

■ Stay in the best of health. Get a physical exam from your personal physician every one to three years, even if you feel healthy.

■ Consider reading the signs more accurately. Try to avoid getting swept into the issue of poor health, but remember that the stress of this trap is truly great enough to make anyone ill.

PUSH-OUT BY
DIMINISHMENT

The next area to look at is the taking away of important aspects of work in order to instigate the process of removing someone from their job.

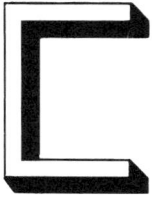

AN ALBUM
OF
SMALL TRAPS

Cold Shoulder. This is finding out that a meeting important to your work took place and you were not invited. Sometimes you find out from an innocent fellow employee who wonders why you missed the meeting. Other times you receive a memo that details decisions that took place at a meeting you knew nothing about.

A more direct form of Cold Shoulder is to miss one too many raises. There is the sense that something must be wrong, but nothing is said. People who miss their second chance for a raise often begin to worry that there are things about themselves that are not right or acceptable. Most Cold Shoulders offer little hope and lots of feelings of entrapment.

The Twilight Zone. You return from a trip to discover that your office has been moved to a less prestigious location. You walk into your office and discover that your leather layback chair is now vinyl stiffback. You sit down and put your hand on a new cold metal desk, not your solid oak, or even walnut veneer, old one. That ashtray, was it different . . . maybe smaller than your old one? You go to turn on the air conditioner and discover that there is a new one in the window, 5000 Btus smaller than your old one. There is a small handwritten note on your desk asking you to use the bathroom one down from your usual one. Have any one of these things been happening to you? If so, you are in the Twilight Zone. These sudden secret changes of your environment are material clues of a definite Push-Out. What you have to determine is just how far out you've been pushed.

Dungeons and Dragons. You, alone, were asked to return the master key that allowed you to open all the doors on the way in to your office. In its stead you were given a key for each individual door. A variation of this is that your key was taken away with the explanation that there was a better way for you to get into your office. Then a new path was revealed to you, with different corridors or doors, that proved your office was closer to the outside world then you thought. It was easier to get in because there was always some secretary, or the custodian, to let you in. (Do you get the feeling here that the Dungeon Master can always come up with an answer to your protests?) Maybe you were told there wasn't a reason for you to have any keys. Maybe your strongest protest could be you might need to get in on weekends. Did you get a thin smile letting you know that they didn't expect you to work extra time?

Dry Breast. Someone informs you that a decision has been made to cut back on your use of expense accounts, credit cards, company-owned planes, company-sponsored club memberships and/or vacation hideaways. You rarely are told by whom, because nobody wants to be the bad parent. You possibly were told that this was part of a general austerity measure, but that explanation wilted after you heard two employees hooraying over their upcoming, company-paid trip to the California health spa.

ANALYSIS

WITHHOLDING TO AVOID,
LOCK OUT, AND DEPRIVE

There is not a real lot to say here. Most of these reductions seem like taking candy from a baby. There are many ways that companies send signals to their employees that they are appreciated. When the signals are withheld or withdrawn, it is quite reasonable to assume a diminishment in status within the corporation. The issue is just how significant are the messages and how small and insignificant does someone get when those privileges associated with the messages are taken away. The answer is indefinite; however the message is clear: the trap has been set.

COPING

WITH DEPRIVATION

■ Do not express or reveal your disappointment. Remember that these decisions regarding your status within the company have been made and expressed without consulting you.

■ Use these direct communications as an opportunity to honestly review your own work performance. Do not lie to yourself now. There still may be a chance of saving your job.

■ Approach your boss with no mention of the material losses. There's to be no crying over spilt milk or lost candy. Ask for a detailed appraisal of your work performance. It is preferable to get this in writing. This ought to give you a good understanding of how you are doing. Be sure to follow through on the criticisms and discuss them with your boss. If there is nothing in writing, there may be nothing to work on (it might be too late).

■ Consider other employment before things progress. Do this quietly and discreetly. Do not do this because you are angry about losing the perks or because of subsequent fair criticisms. Do it because your intellect has made it clear that there is a trap close by and you sense it may be unavoidable.

BENT FORK

There are two kinds of Bent Forks at work: one material and tangible, the second symbolic and emotional. Both Forks represent significant losses and quite painful ways of signaling employees their jobs are in jeopardy. The first example is how the withholding of important work tools is a clear signal of a job in jeopardy.

George was two-thirds through compiling a huge bibliography for the university library. Fifteen years at this job and he had never had a project go on for such a long time. One day his secretary walked into his office in tears. Outside were two maintenance men with a valid work order. They were taking her word processor across the hall to be used by someone else's executive secretary, leaving her with just a typewriter. George was not new to bureaucracies. Though upset, he knew this was some kind of bungling error. He reassured his secretary, even pointing out to her that the typewriter they gave to her was new. She was inconsolable.

George finally tracked down his boss only to discover that there was no mistake. George was furious. Three hours later, staring into his uneaten tuna fish sandwich, his anger turned into nausea. It finally dawned on him the processor wouldn't have been taken away if the administration had wanted the project completed. If they didn't want the project completed, what did that say about wanting George? He pushed the thought out of his mind.

Back to a much slower paced work he went, for four months that is. Then he and three other library employees were "coaxed" into early retirement. There was no explanation, no goodbye, no party, no watch; just a last day of work with the project still three word processor months away from completion.

The next example represents the withholding of symbols that people need to function adequately at work. Although the story revolves around the secretaries, it is important to note that it is the vice president of sales who gets the Bent Fork.

Beth was secretary to the vice president of sales, Mary. It took her fifteen years of diligent hard work to get there. Sarah worked across the hall as secretary to the vice president of advertising. Sarah had been with the company for only four years.

One day Beth went to ask Sarah a question and saw a plastic and bronze sign on her desk: Sarah Vincent, Executive Secretary. Beth felt upset, and asked Sarah where she got it. Sarah told her that it came from the corporation. Two weeks ago Sarah's boss had told her that she got the new title. There were no changes in duties, nor a raise.

Beth went immediately to her boss, Mary, and asked her how she had been passed up for the promotion. Mary was busy, somewhat distracted, and completely ignorant of Sarah's advancement. Beth told her there was something very wrong about Sarah getting advanced before she did. Her boss told her to stop being jealous and petty. Beth was furious. True, she was jealous, but not as much as she was puzzled. It didn't make sense, and her feelings were hurt.

Her stomach gnawed and grumbled for three days and nights. Finally she picked a time when her boss wasn't busy to discuss it again. Mary was no more receptive then she had been before. Mary felt the new title was unimportant because there was no pay differential. Beth wanted to know why there was no advancement for her. This time Mary got angry and told Beth to stop bothering her. Beth backed off and tried to point out that it was a lot more important than Mary imagined. "Something is wrong here, I'm sure of it," Beth told her.

Two months later Mary came into Beth's office very sad and tense. It seemed that Mary had been transferred. Beth wasn't quite sure how to respond. For two weeks Mary was barely around, then she came in to announce to everyone that she had taken a job with another company. Within six months Beth was promoted to executive secretary in the president's office and Sarah's boss was vice president of advertising and sales.

ANALYSIS
WITHHOLDING IMPORTANT
WORK TOOLS AND SYMBOLS

What is lost in Bent Fork relates directly to the task: a work-related tool or contact that renders someone less able to function. Bent Fork can also be the loss of a company symbol of functioning, a title. The importance of titles is not the content of the words, but the position in the company that the words symbolically denote. These symbols carry immense weight, but they are heavier burdens when lost.

Companies that are close to letting an employee go, but still unable to state it directly, will often use the Bent Fork to send the signal. If the signal is received then it is an opportunity for the company and the employee to save face. It helps avoid a firing and enables the employee to leave with some style. The problem is that the employee who has received the message is forced into a race to move on before getting fired. This has unique pressures all its own.

COPING
WITH GETTING LESS THAN NEEDED
TO GET THE JOB DONE

■ Know the symbols of authority and status in your company that pertain directly to work. This will enable you to appreciate the positive and negative comments that might come your way.

■ Consider your subordinates to be part of your professional career. What they are called and what tools are allocated to them are direct messages about your fit within the company.

■ Work hard on your ability to read between the lines. Some of the seemingly least significant moves a company can make have the greatest career import. There are no generalizations here.

One executive stated that employees in his company could tell who was going to get fired by the freshness of the flowers in their secretaries' offices. It seems that this company allocated the disbursement of fresh flowers by way of the night maintenance crews. Those crews cleaned the offices and then distributed flowers each night according to an organized work list. The work lists were created by the maintenance management team whose manager met daily with the vice president. This same vice president was responsible for all personnel matters as well as plant and ground development and maintenance. Stale flowers in this company had morbid significance.

■ Bent Fork brings up the need to decide whether or not to accept the deprivation and wait for the seemingly inevitable, or resign gracefully. There is no way to cover the ramifications of such an important decision, though later in the book come detailed discussions of the practical matters related to giving up, or losing, a job. Faced with this decision, you should consult a loved one or close friend, and focus on what you will lose and gain from quitting. What will happen to your public image, as well as your private thoughts and feelings about yourself? What is your style of solving dilemmas like this; and, what can you live with the longest? Do you do best walking away from problems or seeing them through? Do you do best in direct or indirect confrontation? What is your past history with events such as this (don't forget similar events, like leaving a sports team, quitting school, leaving a summer job, leaving home, or even stopping attendance at a church or synagogue). Look hard at these past events to give you a clue as to how to handle Bent Fork.

■ If a direct Push-Out comes your way, go straight to management with a cool head and begin a dialogue about your career performance and the company's goals for you. There is no need to bring up the clues you used to ask for the meeting. It is better for you to appear to be taking your own initiative than to be reacting to the company.

It is always better to respond to the implication that there is a problem than to take issue with the particular events that signaled the existence of the problem to you. Find the energy to persevere at work; and, in a parallel fashion, approach management showing your own initiative and interest (rather than worry and concern).

PUSH-OUT BY
ABUSE OF FEELINGS

MICKEY
MOUSE

In Mickey Mouse you are told to do things at work which demand very little of you, your abilities, or your knowledge. It may be that your usual work is being diverted so that someone else will shine. It could be that you took the wrong job in the first place. When you do that, you set yourself up.

In its more subtle forms, Mickey Mouse is a Set-Up for termination. As a Set-Up your job could have drifted below your skill level because you grew and the job didn't. Or, maybe your boss is afraid you will look too good, or is trying to bore you right out of work. Anybody who enjoys a Mickey Mouse job is caught in a Termination Trap.

Mickey Mouse renders you vulnerable to being fired for lack of initiative, unproductivity, or inability to grow and change. There is no adequate defense for not functioning or producing at your expected level. It is possible that Mickey Mouse can be created to either bore someone into quitting or to prove that they aren't working very hard. Yet, there are times when companies really don't have work for employees. If that situation persists, when the inevitable layoffs come, the contented person with the Mickey Mouse job is often the first to go.

The one exception to the above is in the situation where you and your employer know that your abilities far exceed the job requirements but that you have contracted to perform the job at its present level. In this situation your employer expects to have disgruntled employees with lots of complaints and high employee turnover. This is often called "Summer Job" by college students waiting tables on the Vineyard or "Private First Class" by a high school graduate in Army basic training.

COPING
WITH BOREDOM
ON THE JOB

■ Be certain that you are in a Mickey Mouse situation. Check with your boss about the nature of your assignment. Ask for a written job description when you are hired . . . (next time!).

■ Avoid sitting back and resting when in a Mickey Mouse position. Complain gently about it and ask for more work. If none is forthcoming find some that is directly beneficial to the company. Be certain that this work is cleared by your boss (after you have begun it).

■ Consider using the time to advance your training and knowledge. Again be sure your boss knows that you are doing this.

■ Put guilt on your side. If there is any chance your skills have been ignored when you were told to do nothing important, you may be facing a potential Push-Out. Keep memos of record. Be careful not to break company rules and regulations. Show initiative and energy at all times. At the least this will help with negotiating for severance and unemployment insurance. Maybe it will keep you from getting fired.

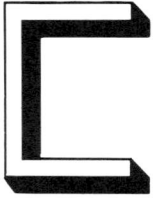

THE DILUTION SOLUTION

No example necessary; you are simply told that the company is undergoing a reduction in force (RIF), and you are part of the force being reduced.

ANALYSIS

YOUR JOB IS
WITHHELD FROM YOU

This could be a corporate-wide decision. It could be your division. It could be just you. No matter, this is the clearest of all the direct signals of getting fired.

COPING

WITH WORK FORCE
REDUCTIONS

■ First determine if your seniority, or retention rating was computed properly. Is your number (ranking) in the corporation up? Be certain that no one is miscomputing your rating in order to move you out selectively.

■ Decide if you're going to fight a miscalculation (whether intentional or not). Be sure to hire a lawyer just at this point. If you decide to fight and you lose, could you be dismissed on the basis of charges stemming from your fight? Losing a fight like this could cost you your pension and insurance coverage.

■ Be careful about accepting a downgrading into a position soon to be abolished. Many RIFs are designed to move people into the position where it will be easier to let them go entirely. This occurs most often in government jobs.

■ You have to study the consequences of every move as if you were already fired. See later in the book for detailed discussions on how to handle the specifics of getting fired.

INDIRECT PUSH-OUTS

The final Termination Traps are the Push-Outs that put pressure on everyone. These indirect, or generalized, Push-Outs may apply to only a select group within the organization, but the implications are corporate-wide. These Push-Outs are based on management decisions that often are quite far removed from your immediate boss. There may be a company policy to phase out people over forty-five to fifty-five years old who are involved with jobs that demand high energy. There may be a directive to remove people who have marital problems from positions of responsibility.

Sometimes job descriptions have been written to both hire you and then later move you out of a job. This style of using a diffusion of management decisions in order to manipulate people's careers makes it more difficult for the individual being pushed on to know how to respond in a productive manner. The basic point is that if important matters related to individuals' careers can be imbedded in the administrative tone and style of a company, then no single manager ever has to feel responsible for pushing someone out. Managers can just say: "Oh, that's the way we do things here," or "This is the way the company is run," without being held accountable for the pressure being applied to push someone out of a job. This is another example of "the whole being greater than the sum of its parts."

TRAPS
FOR OLDER
EMPLOYEES

Older employees are often victims of Indirect Push-Outs. The present trend to distribute a finite amount of work among a larger number of people has led to earlier retirements. Thus it is not so easy any more to call early retirement a true retirement.

Primeval Sloop. This is one way companies have of moving older people out despite nondiscrimination laws. You may be presented with the dilemma in a corporate memo 1) asking people to accept special packages to retire early; 2) suggesting that employees use sick time in their negotiations for early retirement; or 3) simply declaring a change in the benefits schedules to influence retirement decisions. You may first notice the problem when you unconsciously feel pressured to read the company personnel manual, or examine your retirement benefits.

Condemned Land. This is a government move where a piece of property is needed in order to "benefit all of society." The particular governing body then makes the owner an offer for the land. This offer always is difficult to refuse because there is always the fear that refusal might lead to expensive legal hassles, a withdrawal of the offer, or condemnation (of all kinds).

The same mechanisms apply when corporations want employees to exit early and make offers to facilitate the Push-Out. Often a clear sense of urgency accompanies the offer, leaving the employee feeling there may be more to lose in not accepting the Push-Out. Naturally the company has its own goals, some of which may be the genuine welfare of its employees. However, the criteria for determining the "best good" for someone else are often distorted by the needs of the company determining that "best good."

COPING
WITH BEING TOLD YOU'RE
TOO OLD TO WORK

■ Read your company manuals. Review your pension plans. Seek private and/or union legal advice.

■ Suggest meetings with employees who fall within similar Push-Out potential.

■ Review your job performance by pulling out all the job appraisals you have kept. Sit down with your boss and review the present quality of your work. Get a feeling for any possibility that downgrading your next appraisal may be part of the pressure to get you to consider taking the next Primeval Sloop ride out the company's door. Ask for a memo documenting that meeting with your boss, and be sure to keep your own notes.

■ Be certain to involve your family in these discussions. Part of the stresses of early retirement that the company cannot consider when it works up an offer is how things stack up in your personal life. Only you can assess how much better it will be for you to be home earlier than you or your spouse had counted on.

■ If technological change is creeping up on you, consider either job retraining (with company sponsorship or on your own) or job change.

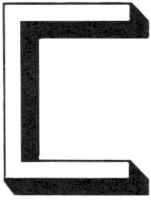

MORE PUSH-OUT TRAPS

The following are examples of company moves that are visible and quite obvious. They are lumped together because these moves often appear together in clusters or groups. They rarely occur alone.

The Last Roundup. One day your section and/or division is visited by upper levels of management normally not in your division or section. These are not consultants, they are full-time company employees. They are just there, and everybody feels herded together. The visit is punctuated by direct criticisms or suggestions that leave some people sliced out of the herd for special branding. There are no explanations for the visit, nor are there clarifying or supportive statements from your boss. These managers just come, then they go. The one major clue that this is a Last Roundup is the shared discomfort throughout your immediate work force.

The purpose of The Last Roundup is to do to people what is done to cattle just before the slaughter: round them up and force them into a compromised position. In corporate terms this means exerting informal authority to send people the signal of what is going to happen before the formal decision to let them go has actually been made. It is a move of power and clearly signals that the boundaries of the herded section are not protected. The greatest likelihood is a corporate reorganization or major leadership change. The major consequence is that jobs may be terminated.

The New York Yankees. Has your company recently hired a new manager anywhere above you in the chain of command with a reputation for being aggressive and hard-driving? Has this person indicated openly that he or she is going to pick and choose, maybe purchase, his or her own team? There is a self-explanatory trap here.

Mayflower. Word has it that the company is planning a relocation. The message may be only a rumor, or it can be a documented fact.

Companies often use the Mayflower to move employees out. First comes the announcement of the reorganization, usually long enough in advance to allow those people whose personal life takes precedence over the company to figure out a way to switch jobs. Then comes the company's offer to place those people who don't want to make the move. Along with this are selective restrictions on moving expenses or help with house sales. Lastly, for those who don't get the message, personnel or management can become involved in counseling those who are having difficulty with the transition. This last move is reserved for those who want to stay with the company in its move and don't realize that the company doesn't want them to come along.

Fiddler on the Roof. It is not unusual for corporations trying to make personnel shifts to let their competitors and headhunters know that it is fair to take a look at so-and-so. This is a frequently used method which many corporations deem a humane way to get rid of unwanted employees. It usually happens in the following way. Within the same short period of time several people in the company are approached by headhunters recruiting them for other jobs outside the company.

The Fiddler on the Roof could approach only one person also, but in this form it is more difficult to assess your own company's role in making the new marriage.

The Girdle. Has there recently been a merger within the company, or between your company and another? Is there any chance there is not enough office space or work for the merged teams?

Sincere Sinecure. Some companies have an informal, but very powerful, Push-Out policy which states that family members (or people with any unique preferred status) can move quickly and easily to positions within the company. Simply and inelegantly, the owner of the company's son or daughter will soon be graduating business school. This is less elegant for you the closer your authority is to the boss (owner) and the fewer sections or divisions there are in the company.

Friday Fish Fry. Your boss suggests that you and he get together on Friday afternoon for an important, private, or personal discussion. This is an irregular occurrence and something suggests the possibility of a Termination Trap.

The Royal Flush. Did a recent court decision suggest a divestiture of your division? A variation of this is called Lost Socks. In this situation you just happen across a long-range plan for the company and can't find your task or product anywhere.

COPING
WITH BEING
SHOWN THE DOOR

■ Sit down with your boss and discuss the particular issues. Avoid emotional displays. You need your boss on your side, and there is always the possibility that your boss is on the way out, too.

■ Consider basic survival mechanisms outlined earlier. Most of what has happened here can only be dealt with in general.

■ You can opt to miss the appointment for the Fish Fry and elect to get fired on Monday. At least on Monday there is less chance for getting locked out of your office and more chance for mobilizing crucial survival mechanisms outlined later in the book.

The above examples reveal how individuals can find themselves in situations that cause reactions to vague corporate philosophies. The vagueness is precisely what makes the impact so widespread and powerful. No single individual manager ever feels heavily accountable or responsible for pushing someone out "because this is the 'way' things are done." This same vagueness protects the company also. The employees expect it to happen, are not surprised by it, and therefore don't usually complain. This happens because while belonging to the company the person internalized its moral (and amoral) customs, rituals, and mores.

DIRECT AND TO THE POINT

There are new ideas about employee rights and getting fired which have yet to be put into practice. Many of the new ideas have to do with changes in the law as well as changes in the shared responsibilities between all levels of labor and management. There is a humane and considerate way to establish the causes of, and means for, firing someone.

The following method is presented as an ideal way to be fired. It isn't terrific that you were fired (or could be), but if this is the way it's done, then there's hope for some emotional and professional salvation.

Your company has formal firing procedures with progressive discipline leading to getting fired. You get a formal warning with a probationary period if there are problems in your job. As part of this warning you get copies of previous written warnings, specific areas targeted for improvement, the time period for probation, and a clear statement that this is a final warning. Here are the steps.

1. Your manager comes to you with a frank, negative work appraisal. Your boss is calm, understanding, and firm. This first meeting is informal, but it is clear that the facts have been checked, maybe even double checked. Your boss has not waited to tell you, most of the data is fresh and to the point. From this point on, further complaints are written down and sent to you.

2. You have ready access to internal grievance procedures, and your company makes these open and available to all employees. As part of any problem you have with work or work assessments, these procedures take into account your personal life, health, and any financial difficulties you may have.

3. Your side of the story can be told informally in a meeting with people from different levels of management. Someone takes accurate notes and submits a copy to you for your additions and corrections. You don't have to repeat your story to many different bureaucratic levels to get it heard.

4. You do not receive any standardized forms in response to your job problems. Your company is likely to give you human contact when discussing these painful matters.

5. The company is consistent with current and past practices for all employees in your equivalent position. You know you are not being made a special case; and you are certain that the company's alternatives of discipline have been exhausted.

6. You sense that when people above you in the company make a mistake they can admit it.

7. There is a clear sense of finality with a clear decision and full explanation, once the facts are known and presented to you.

8. The company seems invested in your further advancement elsewhere. They may be exporting you, but they want others to see you as a positive product of the years you spent with them.

It is no fun getting fired, let go, or unwillingly retired; but, the above method creates an atmosphere of fairness and clear thinking. Should getting fired have to happen to you, hope that it happens in the best possible way.

7

WIN, LOSE
OR DRAW
SURVIVING A SET-UP
OR PUSH-OUT

There are personality factors and experiences which can help or hinder your adjustment to the threat of being Set-Up or Pushed-Out. Termination Traps are scary and sometimes seemingly unbearable. The intensity of your discomfort will be influenced by the power of the company's signals, as well as unique things about your personality that resonate with the pain of potential job loss.

THE ABILITY TO
HANDLE LOSS

Losing a job is a real loss, the kind that causes hurt, grief, pain, denial, anger, and depression.

All losses hurt, and they always leave us changed people. We all carry with us feelings, attitudes, and beliefs from past losses, such as death of a loved one, a parent's divorce or our own, illness, graduations (where one leaves behind the life of a student), death of a pet, geographical moves. We tend to fall into old ways when dealing with new experiences. For example, losing a parent when one is young can leave a person very vulnerable to the emotional effects of future losses because the old feelings can be called forth each time there is a new loss. These are losses which leave indelible scars and weaknesses making future losses less bearable. Someone who suffered through the death of a father in childhood may unwittingly respond to male authority figures as potential replacements for the dead parent. In this position, that person is especially vulnerable to potential rejection and less capable of handling job losses. A child who lost a parent and coped by retreating into a fantasy world may, as an adult, use the same protective mechanism and have difficulty facing the reality of the signals coming his or her way. A third child who experienced the death of a parent with the support of grandparents and teachers might be prepared later in life to face impending job loss by falling back on a family as well as a reservoir of problem-solving capabilities.

IS LOSS PARTICULARLY
PAINFUL FOR YOU

Now's the time to examine your ability to handle losses by taking a look at your past experiences. Were there times in the past when you experienced a loss from which you had trouble recovering?

Some people cannot watch Walt Disney movies because of unresolved earlier losses of pets. Some people avoid saying good-bye when leaving friends because of difficulties with losses. There are people who cannot go to funerals, others who avoid new friendships, and people who fight and get angry as a way of saying good-bye. These people have signs of potential difficulty with loss. Are you one of these people?

Are you still grieving for somebody, or something, lost? Do you have recurrent problems in situations that have loss as a part of the experience? Are there occasions that evoke unusually strong feelings inside you? If so, talk this over with a family member, friend, or professional.

One particularly difficult complication from loss is prolonged grief. The signs of this extend from persistent chronic depression to the superficially positive (but underlying sad) overdeification of a lost person or pet. If prolonged grief is your problem, do you know that you are very vulnerable to future losses of all kinds? The best way to work on prolonged grief is to find someone who is good at listening, sharing, and understanding—all in a nonjudgmental way. Look to family or friends who were not caught up in the grieving event, clergy, or mental health professionals. Prolonged or delayed grief are two important past events that can have a profound effect on the way people handle any work situation. Go for help with this one.

Have you had a series of losses in the last five years (health, moving, death, illness, job)? If so, you should expect some increased difficulty handling work losses, no matter how "clear your head" is.

There are ways you can train yourself to handle difficulties with loss better, but the best training methods vary from individual to individual. For example, if the loss of a prior job, years ago, has left you distrustful of managers, then a way to handle this problem is to first examine your present work relationships. If you, or someone you have discussed this with (like a friend), note that there are problems, then it may pay to consult a professional. Some people in this situation have actually been able to go to their personnel directors and openly discuss their past difficulties and ask for assistance in their present job. In the appropriate environment, this establishes the employee as open, honest, and wanting to change for the better. This kind of employee is always a rare and valuable find for any company; and more and more companies are learning to appreciate people who approach problems in this way.

LIMITATIONS TO
FINDING OTHER WORK

There may be few jobs available because of circumstances in the economy. Factors such as population and geography may limit other work opportunities. The skill level and experience demanded in the job market may leave you underqualified now. Is your age a limiting factor? (Despite federal regulations, there still are multiple opportunities for employers to pass up aging job recruits.)

Unfortunately, the real or imagined lack of other work opportunities creates a forced attraction to your present job, even when it is in jeopardy. This pull toward the job, combined with a Set-Up or Push-Out, will certainly increase the tension. After all this pessimism, it is worthwhile to remember that your confidence sags after your job turns sour. No matter what your age or health, it is probable that the opportunities for work are greater than you think. One way to minimize limitations to other employment is to consider the following suggestions.

■ Always keep your eyes and ears open for other work. It never hurts to keep your horizon as broad as possible.

■ Analyze the skills you brought to the job, and those you developed on the job. Be sure to look at what you actually do at work (rather than what your title is). You might be surprised that you have capabilities which transfer readily to careers different from what you are presently doing.

For example, a postal clerk of twelve years duration was excellent at fast hand-sorting of mail because of her logical, meticulous way of handling tasks plus her excellent memory. She survived the tension of a threatened job loss by turning her skills to a computer programming course at a local community college. Eventually she left her job for a professional position as a computer programmer with an accounting firm, paying over twice the salary of the Postal Service.

■ Consider using a hobby, or special talent, to run a small cottage industry. There are many regularly employed people with small-scale businesses making furniture, repairing electric or gasoline motors, growing vegetables and fruits, and raising animals. Making good money from a small hobby is not just a financial cushion. The self-esteem and positive feedback that one derives from doing something well is truly priceless.

PHYSICAL OR EMOTIONAL LIMITING FACTORS

Your constitutional makeup dictates what types of employment are most suitable for you. This is most obvious to those who have become ill while working and are left with a mild disability which renders their skills less marketable with another company. In the first company they had skills plus knowledge about how the company functions. To a strange company, they have only the skills, which are often overshadowed by the disability.

If you have become physically or emotionally disabled since the start of your job, it is difficult to know whether or not to tell the company you are working for (or any future employer). Check with your doctor to have a current understanding of any disabilities. Also, check with a lawyer about your rights at work, if (or when) you are fired. The laws are even more complex than the feelings about this issue.

THE INFLUENCE OF AGE AND EDUCATION

How old you are, your experience, and level of training are critical variables which will influence your feeling that you can survive the potential loss of your job. A lot can be done about education, providing there are the motivations and resources. There is little that can be done about the inexorable marching of time.

Consider taking courses at your local secondary schools, community colleges, or universities. There are always correspondence courses. This is certainly easier said than done; however, it feels terrific once you do it. If you find yourself blocked when trying to move in this direction, then you might consider visiting classes with a friend, walking around the campus, even writing for catalogs or going to your local library. (Do you know how nice it can be to discuss education and learning with librarians?) Consider auditing a course without the pressure of grade performance. Try joining informal learning groups such as crafts, bridge, music, or dance groups, just to reassure yourself that you can still learn and grow. It also helps to experience the togetherness of a focused group.

AVAILABLE SUPPORT SYSTEMS

Turn to people and special interests for solace. Misery doesn't really love the company of more misery, it needs the company of comfort. Adequate supports can extend from family or friends to membership and a sense of belonging in other groups such as clubs, sporting teams, religious organizations, and even neighborhood bars. But remember, your need to avoid alcohol and caffeine is more important than ever.

YOUR FEELINGS OF
SELF-CONFIDENCE

Without self-confidence, coping with the Termination Trap is almost impossible. How to get it (and keep it) is worthy of a book in itself. You cannot feel self-confident without being "in training" all of the time. Being in training means constantly building your self-confidence by keeping yourself open to new and challenging experiences; avoiding a narrowing of your coping skills which so easily can happen when security comes first; and, keeping an honest self-accounting that allows for your own personal changes and growth.

DEFENSES WHICH
HINDER COPING

Neither denial nor excessive worry will help you cope with potential job loss. A certain amount of "worry-work," focused on the present and future, is necessary to mobilize a strategy for survival. Denial serves to shut out the unpleasantness in the present and temporarily can be quite comforting. Yet denial also shuts out planning and coping behaviors so necessary to cope with Termination Traps.

Excessive worry results from certain underlying personality traits such as over-awareness as well as a tendency for detailed and grinding thinking. There is not a lot that can be done to change either of these when you are under stress. But if you are generally meticulous and/or unusually watchful, then consider some hard work on how to relax. You might try regular exercise, meditation, or relaxation exercises.

Illusions of invulnerability, that feeling that nothing can or will go wrong, are also quite comforting, but entirely unrealistic. Feeling invulnerable is one tiny step beyond feeling rightfully confident. One must always know the difference. When Richard Nixon was caught in Watergate, he went on television to protest the innocence of "The President." He had wrapped himself so tightly into the role that he confused himself with the job of being president. Holding this constitutional position up for everyone to see gave him an illusion of invulnerability behind which he, the person, tried to hide. It is not unusual for people to insulate themselves from particular stresses in their jobs by creating and maintaining the illusions that "it can't happen here" in my job.

The most primitive defenses against the threat of getting fired actually render the person more susceptible to the event. The most common one people employ when their job is threatened is to dig in and do what they've been repetitively doing all along. No matter that these same behaviors may have contributed to the job jeopardy in the first place. People relying on rituals to cope with stress continue to behave the same way as before, only now more often. It is a rule in human behavior that a person under stress is most likely to fall back on old behaviors to solve the problem. If the person has learned useful ways of coping with potential loss and stress then this is what will be used. If they have not developed a repertoire of coping behaviors then the trap is more intense; the solutions to getting out more difficult to find.

USEFUL GENERAL ACTIVITIES
FOR COPING

There are useful activities you can practice every day no matter whether your job is going smoothly, you've just maneuvered out of a Set-Up, or you are in the midst of being Pushed-Out.

Treat Yourself as Indispensable to Your Own Well-Being. The person who is most responsible for what happens to you in the long run is you. You may not be total master of your fate; none of us are. But if you had to hire and manage someone whose job it was to run your life, how would you treat that person? Well, that person is you. It is shocking how few people look at their own lives as being their own.

Cherish Your Personal Life. Whatever is important to you personally should take precedence over work. If you don't treat yourself well and respect yourself for doing it, don't expect others to do it for you. Skipping vacations, missing personal engagements with close friends, forgetting hobbies, taking a marriage for granted are all ways to diminish your personal life.

Putting work first is different from integrating a work experience into your cherished life. When you work for a company there are always a certain number of things you are expected to do that only serve to keep the company alive. People in companies know that a lot of what they do protects and serves the organization, not just the task of the company. If companies cherish themselves enough to expect their employees to protect the organization, then don't you think it's wise for you to be doing the same thing for yourself?

Any weak link in your personal life is a potential Set-Up at work. At the very least, if your personal life isn't going well, you will be inclined to expect too much from work. You will need too much from work, and it will have too great a leverage over you. Your ability to handle even an innocuous Set-Up is then terribly compromised.

Consider Your Job as Always Totally Expendable. No matter what your work and economic situations are, it is still possible to live with the attitude of not putting "all your eggs in one basket," in the sense of both emotional and financial commitments. Consider developing new nonjob-related skills on the outside, preferably in an area that gives you great personal expression and pleasure. Of course, this is more difficult for people living from one paycheck to another. Remember that your attitudes about how flexible you can be are dependent on how open you are to change throughout your life, not just when you have to change.

Your Intimate Relationships Should Be Supportive. If you want to build a truly helpful support system, you must work on giving and receiving. You will need to develop abilities to ask directly and gently for what you want. At the same time you should appreciate that giving something to someone else means the most if they get what they want.

Be careful to nurture your close relationships at all times. They are precious and quite fragile. Remember that some people tend to abandon them during times of stress because of panic, shame, guilt, or denial. It is hard to deny what is happening to you when you are around someone you are usually very honest with. Allow for open, unstructured time to talk, face to face, candidly, seriously, and deeply. If your relationships allow for expressing feelings openly, then accept and expect anger, tension, and fear without surprise, shock, or your own withdrawal. These are feelings, too. Acknowledge and reward all expressions of feeling from your spouse and expect the same in return. This will help you build a useful support system for the future.

Recognize Your Personality Traits. Given the competitive, high-energy, product and task orientations of organizations, watch for any signs of changing into a high-performance machine, a Type A person. It's potentially life endangering. A Type A person is considered to be at greater risk for coronary artery disease than a Type B person.

Are you a Type A? Type As have firm resolve, act with decisiveness, have unswerving self-confidence, and they are heavily inclined toward hard-working perfectionism. Type As are always on time, tend to smoke cigarettes, and wait for almost nothing. Vacations are for "doing things," not relaxing. Rarely do Type A people feel tired. Their physical health is good right up to their heart attacks, though they have little time for exercise other than bending their elbows. They often know little about feeling tense or afraid, because when these feelings happen, Type As are very quick to do something about the feelings, even before they are experienced. Thus Type As fidget a lot; but when confronted with how tense they appear, they will deny it and report, "I was only thinking," or "No, I'm not tense, just trying to figure something out."

Type A people are just what most companies want: somebody who is always doing something. When Type As go to a store, they take journals with them to read. Everything is a game with a method of scoring that Type As try to figure out. Each scoring opportunity offers a chance to get more points toward winning. Type As are not particularly easy to work for or with. They want respect and little else. The bonds they form at work always mean business, and they drive themselves ruthlessly.

Type As get fired because they know so little about feelings. They are let go usually for reasons of personality clashes, not poor task performance. Type As are quick to anger, slow to fire someone else; they are resolved in their quest for the Holy Grail of competition and big numbers.

Type B people are equally bright and competent, equally serious, but more easygoing in manner, able to enjoy free time, and rarely inclined to display impatience. Type Bs may get the ulcers, but not the heart attacks. Although few Type As will admit it in psychotherapy, they seem afraid of the Type Bs quiet togetherness. Type As proclaim little respect for Type Bs. They usually blame them for getting in the way or slowing things down. There is an anger that surrounds a Type A person which just isn't there with a Type B. Type As seem to bristle with, and rave at, Type Bs. Type Bs seem to use

Type As. Type As need to work especially hard on expressing their emotions in words because their high performance will not necessarily overcome that deficiency.

Who is it who has risen to the top of your company, A or B? It appears to me that there are more Type Bs in the upper levels of management. If you are a Type A, you won't want to think about that. Type As need to change, for reasons of health as well as employment. Type Bs seem more medically sound. It would appear that the tortoise will always beat the hare!

Keep a Running Account of Yourself. By this I mean consider using self-reflection and discussions with family and friends to keep current with who you are and what you are accomplishing. It is a good idea to be willing to write these thoughts down and update them at least once a year. This will be helpful in exposing your weaknesses to yourself, before they become an issue at work.

When keeping your account of yourself use the following criteria. Use your own words to describe yourself with the following list as a guideline. Then sit down with someone who knows you really well and ask them to read over your assessment. This may help clear up underassessments and overassessments on your part. It also might help you develop a more descriptive vocabulary (and appreciation) for your strengths (people generally tend to underrate themselves). Here is the list. Consider commenting on your strengths and weaknesses.

- Personality
- Potential
- Adaptability
- Health
- Ability
- Education

The next set of variables has to do with certain management capabilities. Are you good at:

- Estimations
- Future planning
- Organizing others' plans
- Giving orders
- Assessment and evaluation
- Coordination of many activities

How much of your knowledge is practical (experiential) and how much is theoretical (intellectual)? Where are your skills:

- Sales
- Writing
- Installation
- Stock control
- Maintenance
- Distribution
- Production
- Technical skills
- Teaching
- Negotiations
- Public relations
- Operations
- Purchasing
- Security
- Design

Do you work best:
- Alone
- In face-to-face groups
- In large groups
- In permanent work groups
- In task-oriented dissolvable work groups

How do you handle work or time that is not programmed and structured?
- Are you an initiator or a reactor?
- Do you make plans or follow others' guidelines?
- Do you find yourself structuring your own free time?
- Do others (your spouse) generally fill up your spare time?

If you find it difficult to create your own self-assessment from the above listing, then please consider using the vocational counseling service at your local state college or university. For a minimal fee, you can take a battery of tests oriented toward revealing your strengths, interests and abilities that tie in with particular vocational areas. It will give you an independent idea of areas you might consider for future employment.

Read Richard Bolles' book, *What Color is Your Parachute* (Ten Speed Press, Berkeley, 1981). This book contains a wealth of information along the lines of self-assessment for particular jobs and types of employment.

Keep an Up-to-Date Assessment of Your Job Requirements. What is it your job used to demand? What skills and knowledge must you have to perform currently? What will you need in the future to keep up with long-range plans and trends?

Make an annual work plan to deal with any deficiency that might increase your likelihood of getting fired. Don't forget the importance of continuing to educate yourself; consider everything from computer courses, business writing courses, to time-management courses. Look into your company's educational reimbursement programs (many go unused because no one knows about them). The time to get training (for advancement, or another job) is when you still have an employer.

Actively Participate in the Social Aspects of Work. Over 75 percent of being successfully employed is the ability to belong to the group. It is important to stay involved with those activities that on the surface do not seem job-related. They are important forms of job insurance. Know these "belonging" behaviors, even if they don't make sense to you yet. Every good boss knows just the right time to throw a party, knows just how to set up the coffee machine, knows just when to suggest lunch on the company to the employees. Consider these events as part of your job, and participate actively in them as if they were an assigned work project. Even where, and with whom, you have lunch has very much to do with keeping your job. It is not possible to emphasize this point too much. Far too many people ignore the importance of these social aspects of their jobs.

Some people find jobs where their personality fits perfectly with the work circumstance. The rest of us must work at belonging and make belonging a part of work. The art is doing this without sacrificing who you are and what you are all about. Remember that doing your job while belonging to the company (not being controlled or owned by the company) is insurance against being fired.

Maintain a List of Lethal Aspects of Your Job. There may be situations or circumstances at work which endanger your physical and emotional well-being. Having this list creates an opportunity for you to make changes within your job. There is also the chance that the list will suggest administrative proposals to be submitted to your boss (carefully). Stress is only one component of the lethality which I am speaking of, but it is the one which will be focused on in this discussion. Poor, or malfunctioning, systems at work will increase your emotional and physical stress. Do you recognize any of these situations?

- Tedious work and poor working conditions
- Lack of recognition for work well done
- Poor relationships with coworkers
- Poor material and personnel resources
- Inadequate time to complete the task(s)
- Management's inability to function during demanding times
- Large and frequent work overloads
- Poor handling of conflict and uncertainty

Sometimes it is the nature of the work, no matter how well it is managed and carried out, that contributes to stress.

- Being responsible for other people (rather than things)
- Having to make many life and death decisions during the course of your work
- Working in law, dentistry, medicine, transportation, science, electrical engineering, high technology, food handling, and/or managing people
- Having a gap between what you've been trained or educated to do and your present job status
- Having a lack of security, support, or stability in your job

Have a Confidant. It's best to have confidants who work elsewhere. It might be nice to have someone at work, but this is always full of potential problems having to do with trust and confidentiality. Choose as a confidant someone who cares about you in ways that have nothing to do with your performance at work.

Seek Outside Help for Any Alcohol or Drug Abuse, Emotional, or Physical Problems. Do not give your organization an excuse for firing you. If you need medical help, do some careful research *before* you use the corporate insurance company. Specifically question your personnel office as to confidentiality. *How many people handle your insurance forms*? Is your boss or office manager copied on all medical expenditures? Does your insurance company send memos to the corporation on all claims with specific diagnoses and the doctors' and/or clinics' names? Do you know of anyone in your company having had medical information used against them in a job dispute?

Know Your Company's Standard Policy for Laid-off Employees. Avoid being ignorant here. Should you ever be forced out you will want to be certain you will be treated according to usual procedures. Before you take a job be sure to check the employee manual for grievance procedures. Do not wait until you are under stress to review these matters.

Know Everything About Insurance and Benefits. Know everything there is to know about extensions of health disability, and life insurance policies. And, have accurate data on severance and unused vacation pay, your pension fund, and profit-sharing. Always have a financial plan for surviving a 50 percent reduction in income. These are all matters which you must keep current on, even if your job is going well. Many people allow their need to be taken care of to get expressed by assuming the company will always do the right thing. Or, some people express their dependency by concluding that these matters are too complicated, and there's no time to learn about them. It may be more comfortable to depend on someone else to know about these important topics, but, if this "someone" fires you, the support will suddenly not be there.

Develop a Multifaceted Personality. Use hobbies, sports, and education to help with job loss, retirement, changes in health, and adjustment to your children growing up and leaving. This ties in with an earlier suggestion, but also deserves to stand completely on its own as an important reminder.

Consider Resigning. You may lose financial benefits contributed by your employer. On the other hand, you avoid having "fired" in your record. This point almost deserves another chapter, but the decision is remarkably similar to getting married or having children. No one can make it for you. Take your new thoughts and some of my ideas and suggestions on how to beat getting fired, then freely consider the benefits and detriments of resigning.

8

TODAY
I LOST
MY JOB
WHEN THE TRAP
SNAPS SHUT

There are a lot of people in our country who have lost their jobs. *The Monthly Labor Review* of March, 1983, reported that 5.7 percent of the civilian work force lost their jobs in 1982. There were an average of 6,268,000 people a month who were unemployed during the course of the year.

Losing your job means that somebody took it away from you against your will. The impact of the loss is painful, and each person will experience it in a very personal, distinct way.

THE TRAP IS SPRUNG

Wendy found herself in a psychiatrist's office sorting through what had happened in the past two days. She had been with a firm for about 2 years. Three weeks ago her boss informed her that her raise for the next contract year was the third highest in the division. She decided to celebrate by taking her first vacation. That, too, was all right with her boss. Her last day of work before her vacation came and went. She was due to spend the weekend preparing for departure on a two-week cruise to Alaska. The next day, Saturday, the mail came to her home. She felt a little apprehensive seeing her company's letterhead on the envelope. Why would they write to me at home? Other things had to be attended to, so she went on with her travel preparations. That night she paused to read her mail.

The letter from her boss was short and sour. "I regret to inform you of our decision to not renew your contract after next year. We (sic) have weighed this decision carefully, and it is our considered opinion that you do not fit in with our company's long-term plans. The opportunity is ripe for you to pursue your career elsewhere. There is plenty of time to work out the details of your transition. Hope you enjoy your vacation . . ."

Wendy had a flood of thoughts as she stood numbly holding the letter. Why does this hurt so much? How could they . . . I thought they cared for me? Am I losing something I love, or is it something else? The thoughts repeated over and over. She stood with the letter for almost two hours, totally dumbfounded. After a sleepless night, one day before she was due to leave on her trip, she called her boss at home and asked to see him. He agreed to meet her at a restaurant for coffee.

She drove very slowly; everything seemed to be going so fast around her. There were sharp pains in her stomach, and a distinct feeling of lightheadedness. Her mind felt like it had melted away, and she found herself repeating the directions to the restaurant over and over. Wendy arrived forty-five minutes late. She had made three wrong turns. When she got to the restaurant she found herself holding the door open for other people, but unable to walk through it. Finally someone insisted she go first.

Inside at the table her boss initially appeared calm. Wendy couldn't control her tears. This public display of emotion was a first for her. She could feel the shame and embarrassment oozing up into her face. He was cool, very distant, and much more fidgity than usual.

Wendy asked him what had gone wrong. Nothing, he replied. Maybe she had forgotten that when she was hired the company had told her it was for three years. But she had gotten that big raise for her third year. He agreed. He even felt her work was terrific; but the company had a policy to keep only one of the five training managers. The person the company decided to keep was "just about the best we've ever seen."

Why had the letter come to her? Why didn't he talk with her about it? Why just before vacation? Wendy was trying to make everything go away by pleading. Her boss appeared shaken and began explaining to her that the other three had gotten their notice the same way, the same day. He went into a long discussion about how he had written her job assessments, all of which had been very favorable. He told her that the decision was not his to make. He did not have any say in who the company chose. More importantly he had just heard what the decision was the Wednesday before. He then tried to tell her that he had hoped she didn't get the letter until after her vacation. That is why he didn't say anything to her. Then he told her how painful the whole thing was for him. He liked her and would write her a good recommendation.

What happened inside of Wendy, her thoughts and feelings, has been experienced in some form by most people who have been fired. It really doesn't matter whether or not the firing is anticipated, or what the specific circumstances are. There is almost always a sense that a trap has snapped shut.

The body's natural defense to the shock of being fired is a progressive decrease in alertness, numbness, poor memory, a loss of contact with one's own feelings, decreased attention span, disconnected thinking, and a difficulty attending to details. This might appear, at first glance, to be a depressing list of responses. It is usual, expectable, and quite normal for the situation. In Wendy's case, Wendy thought she was fine when she ended the meeting. Then she had an accident on the way home and sat in her car refusing to get out. She was brought to the hospital emergency room to talk with a psychiatrist. She could not remember anything about the accident and admitted feeling "dead inside," as if nothing mattered.

Most people experience some physical symptoms when a firing occurs. It is not unusual to have a pounding heart, increased muscular tension, stomach and/or leg cramps, nausea, and a striking initial increase in alertness. For people who are not used to being ill, or for those who are overly preoccupied with their health, these physical responses become their own source of stress. Some people, overwhelmed by the pain of being fired, divert their attention to these bodily signals rather than focus on the real source of pain. Some are inclined to panic and quickly seek medical care.

If these symptoms befall you, do not hesitate to contact your doctor. At the very worst, you will be taking care of yourself; at the very best, you will get a clean bill of health which will serve you in good stead for the upcoming transition.

If there has been little preparation for the event, then there is often a flood of unexpected and contradictory feelings and thoughts. Panic increases. It is very difficult to think ahead, to make plans, or to carry out organized behaviors. Wendy's car accident is not an improbable occurrence. The complexity of a person's responses creates an overload for his or her central nervous systems. It's as if there are ten thousand phone calls trying to jam themselves through a switchboard that is meant to handle one hundred calls. When this happens it is the natural response of the system to shut down.

WHY DOES THIS
FEEL SO PAINFUL

Getting fired is painful because it can feel like you have lost everything. One of the immediate feelings is a sudden, plummeting sense of self-worth. People who lose jobs almost invariably start behaving as if all of society no longer values them—a definite, strong grief reaction. There is an acute sense of vulnerability, like being turned inside-out. For many people, there is a sense of losing control over feelings and thoughts. While time slows down, thoughts speed up; usual senses of oneself quickly disappear. This loss of psychic balance is entirely normal, although it feels wrong, or bad. When you lose a job, you lose a whole series of behaviors and feelings that occur repetitively at least five days a week. The loss is equal to losing mastery over your environment.

Other usual feelings are inadequacy, powerlessness, frustration, a sense of betrayal, and alienation. These feelings are also normal and expectable given the circumstances. However, these are not commonly experienced feelings for most people. This creates the difficult situation where a person is faced with the trauma of being fired *plus* the trauma of having to cope with a whole series of puzzling new feelings. For those Type A men and women who do not connect their feelings to the work environment (or who have trouble admitting to any feelings at all), the flood of feelings that occur at this time can be overwhelming. These people are at great risk for serious complications of stress.

COPING ON THE DAY
YOU ARE FIRED

It would be nice if I could prescribe ten coping behaviors so getting fired wouldn't hurt. The obvious truth is that there are no easy ways around the ensuing pain and difficulty.

The idea is to have a set of behaviors ready to use in case you do get fired. It is very similar to knowing the way out of a burning building so automatically that you won't have to think about it if there really is a fire.

I think, too, you'll find that these behaviors are essentially transferable to other crises when the stress is so great that you need to do something. So read through these several times and think about them in ways that are meaningful to you. As much as possible, let these behaviors become a familiar ready reserve.

■ Do not pretend to the person who fired you that it does not hurt. In fact, if you reveal (in carefully measured doses) that it does hurt without displaying anger, you stand the chance of mobilizing some guilt and doubt in your boss. Remember that it is a fine line between gaining sympathy and provoking irritation in your boss (a person also uncomfortable with what has happened to you). The same manager who fired you and now feels guilty, stressed, and isolated can actually end up being an informal ally in your severance negotiations, if you don't provoke him or her.

■ Don't fuel the fire between you and your ex-boss. You do not want to create an adversarial stance between you and the company. Perhaps it's easiest to keep the tone of any discussions nonvindictive if you don't hold your boss personally responsible—i.e. the company, not your boss, fired you. For the initial time period, these little mental games can help you hold on to some much needed clear thinking in more important areas. Avoid saying anything impulsively. Do not criticize anyone else. It's all right to express your angry feelings, if that feels right to you, but in an impersonal way.

If you feel you cannot control your anger in a meeting with your boss, stop the discussion and ask your boss to have a third person present, somebody both of you trust. Having another person present will help you stay in control (if that is a problem). The person you ask for might be a member of the Board of Trustees, a clergyman, a union representative, or a close friend of yours in the company. If it is a friend, then explain to your boss that he or she is someone you admire and trust and who you were going to talk with anyway. Be sensitive that anyone in the company who sides with you runs the risk of being tainted by your dismissal. Be certain to discuss this with any person willing to be on your side before you make any mention of it to your boss.

■ Almost immediately you will feel a need to "do something," no matter how purposeless, to cope with the numbing disconnectedness. At this point you are most vulnerable. There is an inclination to lean heavily on help from others. Be wary of accepting this from people at work, especially just after being fired. Before you accept any help from the person who fired you, including the suggestion to meet with outplacement experts, you need to be thinking clearly. The less said the better, so *use* the numbness you feel to your advantage. It is okay to be nonresponsive to suggestions, helping hands, and questions during this initial stage. People will understand the numbness as a reasonable excuse.

■ Now go home before making any decisions that might compromise your position any further. What you are trying to do is avoid confrontation and angry feelings at work. These might jeopardize future negotiations. Do not go to a bar. Tell people at work that you have an important personal appointment if you need to provide some reason for leaving. You might consider using public transportation, or having someone pick you up. It's best to avoid inviting an accident by not driving when so stressed. After you leave, find someone who loves you and avoid being alone. You do need to do something. What you should do is tell your spouse, a family member, or close friend the truth.

The truth is not just that you were fired. The truth is also your freshest regrets, nagging thoughts, and guilt about what you think you might have done to contribute to getting yourself fired. At this most vulnerable time you might be less likely to forget whatever your role was in getting fired. Documenting this with someone you trust (to not use it against you) will be very helpful during later stages of negotiating a severance package. It will also be helpful to have someone listen just in case you are blaming yourself too much. Having a loved one listen will give you a quick sense of having an ally. He or she also may be better able to make those kinds of trustworthy suggestions that you can accept at a time when you are so vulnerable.

■ Avoid acting on the inclination to run away. Everyone feels this in one form or another. Fleeing by physically withdrawing in any way sets a dangerous precedent for future life events. It also weakens your position for severance negotiations. Avoid running to alcohol or drugs.

■ Begin to get a sense of how much, and what, you are going to feel comfortable telling to others about getting fired. Hidden in this consideration is the worry about revealing those sticky feelings of shame.

No quick answers for this one; except, there is nothing like a close, warm relationship with someone who openly loves you to help with feelings of guilt and shame.

■ Consider what you will be doing with the anger that exists inside of you. Recognize that it is there. Many people hide this uncomfortable feeling from themselves, not only to escape from the pain, but because they have fears of expressing anger. Some people have never known the luxury of being self-confident enough to even accept they can feel, or be, angry. Any open expression of anger should occur only with people you know and trust. You will need the freedom to say what you feel without being judged or retaliated against. Should you share your feelings openly with an outplacement expert be aware that this person may very well report back to your ex-boss. Keep your feelings within trusted, secure boundaries of caring relationships.

■ Begin thinking about how to discuss getting fired with your children, without undermining their sense of security and unswerving faith in you. This is a matter as complex as any. I remember when my own father was fired from a job during the economic downturn in 1957 (I was in my midteens). The vision of him sitting at the kitchen table, crying and, at the same time, planning how our family would survive, set a valuable precedent for my own coping. That he had sadness, frustration, guilt, and anger plus a firm sense for implementing plans for his (and my) hopes was very reassuring. The point is: you needn't fake emotional strength or absolute confidence to your children. Conveying the ability to handle all the varied feelings openly can be priceless for those people who have unswerving faith in you.

PROTECTING YOUR RIGHTS

Getting fired is so laden with feelings that it's easy to forget one important fact: you have rights that need to be protected. First, there is always the possibility for negotiating the circumstances under which you leave the company. Second, there are legal overtones to almost every aspect of getting fired. Lastly, if you can stand to play ball with your ex-employer, keeping the company on your side will undoubtably get you the most, materially speaking.

The following suggestions are specifically designed to protect your rights during the complex process of leaving a company against your will.

■ Get a dated memo from the person who fired you which establishes what happened to you and why. Have that memo contain a clear statement of why you were fired. If possible ask that prior warning documents, or reports of any charges against you be included. It is very important to do this on the day of, or soon after, being fired. You can not get unemployment insurance if the company later claims that you left voluntarily. This memo might also help with other severance issues, and maybe even with the whole issue of being fired in the first place. If you fear your boss will turn on you, or if he or she refuses to give you a memo clearly stating the circumstances of your leaving, then write a memo-of-record as soon as you get home. Keep the original and send a copy to your boss. This puts you on record as a clear thinker who is carefully and discreetly watching out for yourself.

■ You should now busy yourself reading two things: the company's personnel manual and your contract. If you belong to a union, then read their regulations, too. Now check the company's firing procedures. These pieces of paper are often ignored by most people who work in companies. The fact is, however, they exist for a very important reason: to minimize, or prevent, any single person in the company from acting in an arbitrary, personal fashion.

All people should read their company manuals (and their own contracts) very carefully before taking a job. Those areas which are poorly worded, vague, or nonexistent offer any person with enough power and authority the opportunity to inflict harm on others. As bureaucratic as these manuals seem, and as wordy as they can be, they have hidden within them important procedures and protocols for company behaviors. Sensing where the traps are at the beginning of your job will be helpful throughout your career.

These documents are crucial around the time someone has to leave a company. If one or both of these documents do not exist, your stress level will naturally go up because you are left without much recourse other than your own ingenuity. You won't have much of that on the day you are fired.

You still have recourse if the company behaved arbitrarily with you. Your boss may have reams of data to support firing you, but you may have leverage with the whole company. The morale of those people who weren't fired, as well as the reputation of the company, is at stake if you were treated unfairly, and this information is made public. Your company is aware of that, so should you be. Other employees and outsiders could get interested in your situation, as could unions and maybe the courts. All of these are your leverage.

WHAT TO LOOK FOR IN A
PERSONNEL MANUAL AND WORK CONTRACT

First check to see what the policy is for firing people who have your length of time with the company. Were there irregularities in the way you were fired that do not fit with the stated policy of the company?

Does the company have procedures for dealing with any particular family or health problems that you may have? What rules has the company established for those who had recent time away because of personal health or family problems?

Is there a company procedure for involving top level management in firing procedures? If so, was this followed in your case? The higher up a person resides in a corporation, generally the fewer formal procedures there are for firing that person.

Were you supposed to have been notified of a probationary period?

Were there supposed to have been records documenting your poor performance; discussions about poor performance, and corrective suggestions for improvement? Did you see them?

Does company policy state that you have the right to relocation as part of probation?

Does your company have a set policy for termination interviews?

FIGHTING TO
KEEP YOUR JOB

Fighting for your job can be an option, but it must be a carefully chosen and executed one. If you want to fight for your job consider marching straight into top level management's office. This is the opposite of the prior recommendation to go home. Going straight to the top is an aggressive act, and it takes a lot of energy and clear thinking. Be assertive, do not worry about your trembling voice and hands or your wobbly knees. If you elect this route, you have to go with the drama of it all. It's fair to beg, plead, cajole, negotiate. Ask for probation. Ask for your job. Ask the person to consider that your boss made a mistake. This is your final card. If you play it you must use all the emotional leverage that you have. Otherwise read on for further ways to cope.

THINGS TO THINK ABOUT
TO COPE WITH THE PAIN

Getting fired is going to change you for the rest of your life. It is, to say the least, an unforgettable experience. What you want to do from the very beginning is to establish it as a learning experience. The goal is to be able to look back on getting fired and remember the pain, but also to feel that you've grown and developed. This may seem extremely unlikely to you now; but with a lot of hard work, you really can come out of this experience ahead.

Since you need to do something, get out your pencil and paper and start writing. Don't just read these questions. Force yourself to write down the answers. It might take a day or two, but the results will be useful to you over the next eighteen to thirty-six months. When you have finished, sit down with your confidant and discuss each of the questions. Find out their views and feelings about your answers. Do they feel you've been honest with yourself? Have you made excuses either for yourself or your boss?

How Appropriate for You Was the Job You Just Lost? Don't forget that during high school and college (maybe sooner) family and social pressures created lots of tension about having to work in order to survive, or be accepted, or measure up. In the face of those irrational pressures, just exactly how rational was your choice?

If you are taking the questions seriously your answer ought to be as complete as this: ''I took the job (with XYZ Company) because my parents always assumed I'd be an engineer like my Dad and older brother. All through high school, I played saxophone and dreamed of becoming a professional musician. But, I was also good at math, and when anyone asked me what I was going to 'do,' I always responded with: 'be an engineer'. This always met with others' approval. Being a jazz musician was nowhere near as acceptable, and it eventually became a hobby. Yet, the saxophone earned me all my money to get through college and graduate school! I guess I was sidetracked before I even started this job.''

How Much Personal and Professional Expression Went Into the Job You Just Lost? There is no doubt that if the job was personally and professionally gratifying, if it did allow for expressions of your creativity, then the loss and subsequent emptiness can be devastating. On the other hand, if the job was not conducive to being original and creative, or feeling gratified and interested, then noting these deficiencies now can be of great help to putting the loss into clearer perspective.

Did You Have Unrealistic Job Expectations? When you were a child, did your parents create job expectations without being honest about their own difficult work experiences? Did anyone ever talk of work frustrations or disappointments? Did you ever visit your parents' workplaces? Was either of your parents ever fired from a job?

Can You Consider a New Career. This might be a good time to consider not just another job, but another career. Is there something you always wanted to do with your life that you were especially qualified for? Can you drop your socially conceived notions of yourself to actually accept your strengths? Did your parents acknowledge any of your unique or special abilities that didn't fit their preconceptions about the work they wanted you to do?

Did You Chose to Work in a Corporation to Experience Belonging? By this I mean, is there any chance that personal relationships at work became the major motivating force for keeping you going and producing? Are you grieving the loss of the people more than the loss of the job? If so, do you know how to survive on your own? If you feel you can't make it, will you reach out for professional help? Are you willing to consider continuing your personal contacts by reaching out to some of these people in new ways?

Did You Take the Job You Lost Just for the Money? If that's the case, then what you have just lost is financial security. But for many, work equals money and money equals social status and self-esteem. So what exactly did you lose? How much of your identity had you given over to how other people in the company saw you? Ask yourself what are you going to stop doing, or what are you relieved you will no longer have to do, now that you won't be working there? Did you take that job for the prestige society attached to the financial aspects of the position? How important is that kind of recognition and prestige to you now?

Did your company encourage its employees to have big homes and big cars to lock them into feeling financially dependent on the corporation, so they would tow the line when it came to company policies? Where is the line they wanted you to tow, now? Do you have a financial plan to cope with the change in income? Do you know how to get good financial advice, right now? Will you go ahead and do that?

Did You Have Romantic Illusions About This Job? Review in detail the exact reasons you took this job. Also review the reasons why you stayed with it for as long as you did. This is not easy to do, for it demands honesty and directness. That can be painful. For many of us there can be a large discrepancy between our job expectations and the present reality. These discrepancies develop largely because of romantic illusions and assumptions about the nature and character of our careers. Thus, being a fireman is exciting and dramatic in our heads, in reality it is boring, dangerous, and underappreciated most of the time.

What were the romantic illusions you had about your job? Make a list and try to think back to the illusions you had about the nature of the work *and* the kind of people who did that work? Did you make blanket assumptions about the types of people in particular careers—that is, that doctors are dedicated and humane, teachers love children, the clergy is gentle, wise, and forgiving? The romantic illusions that certain careers are uniquely wonderful are supported by religion, movies, literature, teachers, and our parents. Those illusions could have been wonderful and positive as well as confining. How did you see your personality fitting into those illusions? Were any of them fulfilled? List those events that occurred at work which forced you to drop each of the illusions you lost. What illusions do you still carry with you that have to do with the job you just lost? Do your regrets about the lost job link up with those unfulfilled illusions and missed opportunities?

After getting fired you may be suffering from not just the loss of your job, but the forced expulsion and loss of all those illusions you probably were harboring. Making a list of the romantic aspects of the job that were all in your head will help you separate out the losses that are real from the losses that are part of your fantasy life. Now, for future prevention (there will be another job for you in the future!), list those illusions you have for any other work you have considered doing.

Did Your Job Make You Feel Like "Somebody"? Having been fired, do you now feel like a "nobody"? Are you one of those people who have defined themselves by work? What would you say to someone today if asked "What do you do?" What is your mental photograph of yourself? When you close your eyes to "see" that picture, are you in work clothes, or somewhere else in leisure attire? Do you lose your self-respect and confidence when you are not working?

Did You Love Your Job? Was your love for the job pure and true? Some people do love their work, and the particular job they were just fired from. If you've lost something very special and meaningful to you, the pain and grief will be much deeper, the need for trustworthy emotional support much greater.

Can You Now Acknowledge What You Did Lose? Are you willing to admit you have lost the group, the job, the money, and the security of having a position in society as a reference point? Did you get fired from a work situation where you did belong? Had you adopted behaviors, appearances, and beliefs that fit the group? Have you lost the group, as well as the job? There is so much energy expended trying to belong that once the belonging happens (this is before you were fired) it feels like love.

Are there other people in your personal life with whom you have stable ongoing relationships? If you are all alone, will you consider, now, reaching out for support to a religious group or health professional? Are you self-destructive? If you are self-destructive then now is the time to go for help. Don't wait until your habits or impulses get the best of you.

In thinking about the emotional implications of losing your job, the deeper you look for the answers, the more you will find. What you should do with the answers is to search for problem areas and start the ball rolling toward solutions. Acknowledge the positive realities you tended to gloss over. If you allow denial, pride, prejudices, or any feelings to get in the way of correcting and balancing your course, you can lose an awful lot here. The hardest thing to do with your anger, frustration, guilt, and/or shame is actually to consider reaching out and asking for help. If you get bogged down or bewildered, find someone you trust and ask for help. The worst thing you can do at this point is tough out a losing situation. The best thing you can do is make the best of something horrible by committing yourself to a learning experience.

CHAPTER

9

BOUNCING OFF
THE WALLS
AT WORK
AND HOME
FIRST RESPONSES TO
BEING SNARED

The hours and first few days after getting fired are a lingering continuation of the feelings of being trapped. The apprehension and dread of getting terminated is replaced by numbness, hurt, alienation, shame, and guilt. Everything gets turned upside down during this period. You should not go through this phase at work, though this is a tough piece of advice for those

people on two weeks' or a month's notice. During this time you are frightfully suggestible (anyone would be). No matter how clear thinking you may feel, be advised that this is only a defensive illusion. Now is a time for feeling, not thinking. Feeling should be done in a safe place, with people who care for you. We should take a look at the various responses you might expect.

THE GRIM REAPERS

Getting fired is so painful that one can forget that the person who was your manager has become the messenger of doom. Whatever your view was of that person, or the company, it changes very quickly. Maybe in the past he or she was the strict or precise manager, but now you view your boss as having controlled and dominated you. Maybe you now see the supportive secretary of the past as secretive or undermining once you realize she knew it was going to happen and didn't tell you. Maybe the people who worked for you are now thought of as being part of your corporate demise. Even the task or product changes meaning very suddenly. What was once motivating can now appear very negative.

What do these sudden emotional flipflops mean? They are a form of protection. Getting fired is an assault on your confidence, self-esteem, as well as your values. Your first response is to recoil from the pain of termination. Then comes a need to defend yourself from further pain. Everyone knows the best defense is a good offense; so if you're angry after getting fired, it could be appropriate to the circumstances and to your need to defend yourself from pain. I am not saying that your anger is illegitimate, nor is it wrong. It's just that the vindictive expression of anger, or your hurt feelings, can end up posing more problems than it's worth. For this reason you have to be careful to not share these feelings with people at work. Either deep down, or right at the surface, they will know it's only sour grapes.

LOST SOULS

The early responses to your termination extend out into the company for the other people at work also. The easiest way for people to understand your getting fired is to assume that your behavior was in some way deviant. Apart from graduating or being promoted (and maybe an occasional vacation, or death in the family) there just aren't many other ways to leave a group with its blessing. When you get fired many people will assume that you are totally to blame. This is their way of protecting their continued membership in the group. If you are totally to blame for getting fired then they don't have to worry that the company acted unfairly toward you, or that they personally contributed to your demise. Some people, afraid for their jobs, may shrink from you as if you were contagious. In many ways you are contagious: one firing can signal an organization's intent to make a clean sweep. Those aligning with you would appear to be supportive of you, and therefore, condemning your dismissal. Obviously, too, if the company acted unfairly toward you, then it could act unfairly toward them. So blaming you, not looking at you in the office or hallway, or shrinking away from you is a form of denial and protection for them.

You might find yourself sharing this illusion of total blame with them. If you blame yourself entirely for getting fired, then in a magical way you possess all the means to solve the problem. By blaming either your boss, or yourself, you simplify the process of sorting through the complexities of getting trapped and terminated. Simplifying is an early way to get control of an event you may have had no control over. During this immediate response phase, it is very difficult not to feel guilty and full of shame. The people around you and the person inside you are pointing blaming fingers in your direction, and in many ways it is simply easier to agree.

You are not just severed from the company task and payroll. There is an initial post-firing severe loss of emotional ties to the people at work. Being blamed by them and you sets you apart. Many people toward whom you felt neutrally will now feel more hostile to you only because they are still with the enemy. Some work friendships will feel lost immediately because of the self-protective devices both you and others are using. The barriers will seem enormous. This is the reason I have suggested going home the day you are given notice. This phase will pass because it is based more on feelings than on events. It is too risky to act only on the basis of these feelings.

A FAMILY AFFAIR

If you looked at the people and work organization as a family, you may find their reactions to your getting fired difficult to handle. Even though others at work haven't been fired, they can share your numbness and may even display their own pain and grief. This may seem very supportive. But keep in mind just how complex a family filled with feelings can be. Take Emily's situation.

Emily was fired, bright and early on a Monday morning. She heard unusual hesitancy in her boss's voice; then he informed her that she was fired. Emily was shocked. Though he was management, they had been good friends.

He was a dark silhouette against the bright sun, so she didn't see his tears until he moved toward the door. Within seconds she was by his side consoling him for the tough decision he had to make. He begged her forgiveness and told her he was only doing what he had been told to do. For fifteen minutes she comforted him, until he bowed out the door. Within ten minutes three more of Emily's workmates came in. All of them were crying. Apparently her boss had told them that she was upset. They thought Emily needed comforting, one of them said through her tears. Again Emily found herself reassuring everyone that she was just fine. Besides she had never been much for showing her feelings in public.

A friend asked her to go for coffee, and Emily agreed. In the company cafeteria, Emily felt very tense about the possibility her friend might break down and cry again.

Six hours later, home with her roommate, Emily experienced her own feelings for the first time. By then she was exhausted, filled with everyone else's feelings and very defenseless. Within a few days she was in a psychiatrist's office trying to sort out her angry feelings from all the caring ones. It wasn't just getting fired; it was also losing family. It took her some time to realize just how angry she was with this family; and just how burdened she had been taking care of their feelings about her getting fired. The tension between these opposing forces had been unbearable for her.

MUCH ADO ABOUT NOTHING

Being competent, oriented toward the goals of the organization, reliable, and trustworthy (if you were those) are often considered a form of "job insurance." These are values which are held in very high esteem in our culture. If you had been aspiring toward them and still got fired, these values can become tainted by the misery of self-doubt and dwindling self-esteem. It's difficult to know just what to do with broken values. Hopefully you will throw neither them, nor yourself, away.

Those people who don't question their own values, often direct their anger and doubts toward others. If I was doing a good job, then the person who fired me wasn't. Can I do something about this on the day I am fired?

Maybe the most important bit of work that can get done during this emotional time is to look at how you did function in the job you just lost. If you weren't doing a good job, can you face this fact honestly at a time like this? Probably not, but give it a try. Struggling with this issue will demand support from people who care for you. There will be an inclination to see yourself at either one of the extremes of guilt or innocence.

BEWARE THE JOBBERWOCK

The romance of work is so great that during the time just after being fired, illogical responses from you and your boss are likely. Both of you will be under stress. The following discussion is not intended to turn you away from your own pain by dramatizing your boss's dilemmas, but to broaden your level of understanding about what is happening.

A manager who is faced with making the decision to fire you and/or to carry out that decision is rarely gleeful and happy about it. There may be relief in getting rid of an unwanted employee (if that's what you were), but there is no fun. Usually there is worry and guilt. When a manager lays off people, or fires them, it often means the manager has failed. This failure may derive from having hired the wrong people for the jobs to begin with. There is also the realization of the manager's own shortcomings and how these shortcomings might contribute to someone else's job loss. Firing someone conflicts greatly with ideas of kindness and gentleness that people have of themselves, especially in leadership positions. Lastly, having enough power to take people's jobs away from them puts a person in the position of being the focus of other people's anger and resentment.

These pressures will likely reduce your boss's clarity of thought around the time you get fired. The stresses on your boss can be so great as to put him or her in the position of minimizing further impact. He or she may assume an attacking posture, to push you, as well as the pain, away. Your boss may make suggestions supposedly in your best interests, which really only serve to make him or her feel more comfortable. Your boss may withdraw from you and communicate only by memo, or through someone else, totally ignoring you. For these reasons, it will be difficult for you to trust this person now, or maybe ever again!

Just who you can, and do, trust, becomes a constant concern. You will become quite suspicious because the situation is so adversarial. This is the problem of this immediate response phase. There are so many upheavals that nothing feels the same; old relationships as well as old rules become meaningless. The unwanted gains and losses turn everything inside out. You lose the usual sense of who all the characters are; everything seems to have gone askew.

The immediate loss of the people at work that occurs during the response phase can be exquisitely painful. It isn't just that you were fired. Suddenly you are an outsider. All those actions and feelings that formed the regular part of your workday are stripped from you. Those first few days are numbing because your body, mind, and heart are used to the world one way, and that way doesn't exist anymore. It can feel as if everyone in the whole company has fired you because they still have one another, and you don't have them.

The task of the company and the mechanics of your job lose their meaning. What you may have spent years feeling good about was taken away. During the first few days after being fired, it is difficult to figure out whether or not the job ever really was good. If you decide now that the job was good, then the pain and shame of the loss increases. If you decide that the job was really lousy, then you are faced with regret and resentment that you didn't quit or leave years ago.

The day you are fired rarely signals the last contact with the company. Though bewildered and hurt, there may still be a part of you that doesn't want to leave the company. There is probably still a part of you that can't. There may be an office to clean out, car keys to return, clients or office people with whom you must sort out residual business. There may even be months left yet on your contract. Almost for certain there will be negotiations and clarifications around severance.

So you've been snared in a trap, you've gone home to lick the wound, and now the first day or two of emotional responses have passed. What's next?

10

THE
EMOTIONAL
AFTERMATH
COMING TO TERMS
WITH YOURSELF

The emotional aftermath that follows losing a job can last for six to eight weeks. Those people whose wounds haven't almost totally healed by eight weeks have a great risk of future job disabilities. The first part of this chapter will focus on those emotional and intellectual forces in your life that you are most likely to have some control over. The second part is a look at those behaviors you will need in order to work on the more practical considerations, such as negotiating a fair severance.

It is true that the aftermath of job loss goes on as long as unemployment does. It's also true that the economy and your physical location has a real impact on your ability to find work. If you are looking for sympathy in this chapter, here's a little (xxxxxxx); now let's get on with it. There is no time for more; there is too much emotional and intellectual work for us to do here.

OPEN YOURSELF
UP TO COPING

If you acknowledge what happened to you, if you can face it openly with all of its pain, there are ways to cope. Trying to hide by denying what happened only prolongs your emotional responses. The negative feelings are there with the same stickiness that bubble gum has. You can't make them go away. You have certain choices to make. The best way to begin is to first look back on other stresses in your life which you faced and did not run from.

You can expect a lot of feelings to surface during this time: anger, frustration, guilt, shame, embarrassment, sadness, worry. There can even be positive feelings, such as relief, happiness, and a lessening of tension. One hundred technical professional men who had recently lost their jobs were interviewed in a research project. Forty-eight percent revealed that losing their job allowed them to escape undesirable positions. These men still experienced anguish and pain, but they did reveal themselves to be adaptable and able to use personal support systems. Common negative feelings were powerlessness, frustration, a sense of betrayal, and alienation. You can insure that you open yourself up to coping, rather than shutting down and denying it, by participating in two important things: love and support, and taking care of your physical stamina and health.

LOVE AND SUPPORT

Whether you realize it or not, this termination will change you and your family forever. If you start the response phase by talking with loved ones, their listening and responding can help you keep perspective, deal with negative feelings, focus on the future, and remain resilient. You will need a lot of tenderness and calm from those who care for you while the dust settles. Support now consists less of words and more of just being there. This is a good time to reach out to people with whom you have been out of contact, but feel confidently close to. These renewals can be invigorating and quite supportive.

Reaching out to people who care for you offers you a chance to receive help. Watch for any difficulties you may have accepting people's concern. Make these difficulties part of your discussions with them. As you do this you will be forming a group around you whose informal task is to give you support. Feeling more comfortable with

this kind of sharing is a powerful learning experience which will be useful to you in future work and personal areas of your life. The family and friends who share the experience with you, can provide you with a group identity which was taken away from you along with your job. Don't hesitate to examine what those changes in you are.

CAN MY BODY TAKE IT?

How will you know if you are handling the shock of termination in a constructive way? There are very clear signals if you are not doing well. The strong reactions you had when you were told you were fired should have been momentary. No one can live without great risk to their personal health with that kind of stress present all the time. Within a few days, the extreme bodily responses should have quieted down some. So if, by the sixth or seventh day you are having a half to two-thirds of the following symptoms, consider reaching out for professional help.

Are you reexperiencing the day you were fired by having at least one of the following?

- Recurrent and intrusive remembrances of the event
- Recurrent dreams of the event
- Sudden feelings that the event is recurring because of an association with something in the environment (or some idea you thought about)

Is your responsiveness to the outside world numbed in just one of the following ways?

- Markedly diminished interest in one or more significant activities
- Feeling detached or estranged from others
- Diminished intensity of familiar feelings

Have at least two of the following problems, which weren't present before you were fired, appeared?

- Feeling hyperalert, easily startled
- Having trouble falling asleep, staying asleep, or waking earlier than the alarm
- Feeling unusual guilt
- Having trouble remembering and concentrating
- Avoiding following up on important matters related to severance, financial planning, and/or job searching
- Feeling worse when matters related to work have to be attended to

There is actually a name for the above symptoms and signs. It is called Post Traumatic Stress Disorder. It can occur following any one of the many life stresses that befall us all. When recognized and treated early on, it is rarely a prolonged or difficult condition. Unrecognized, it can become chronic, especially when drugs and avoidant behaviors become a regular part of the person's life. Watch out for these symptoms and signs, and consider discussing them with your family physician if they present themselves to you.

I would expect that you will still feel quite badly for a while, but you should be able to see some improvement, especially if you are busy with family and friends, maybe getting legal advice and working out the full details of your departure from the company. You want to avoid the kind of severe stress that creates a depression with a life of its own. You want to avoid fatigue and physical illness.

Let's examine those things to watch out for that can sidetrack you from growing and changing into a stronger person. It is worthwhile to have pencil and paper at hand. If you write down the answers it will be more difficult to forget your insights. Remember that forgetting is a very convenient way to avoid seeing your own mistakes and errors. Though painful, these insights will give you a sense of control and mastery over your situation. They also offer you the important chance to turn a difficult circumstance into a learning experience for the future. Again, use paper and pencil.

THE JAUNDICED EYE

Worrying about how fair or right your boss was in firing you should be limited to the first day or two. Staying with this worry for too long gives undue power to the boss. This kind of worry leaves you under the control of the person who fired you; it also relieves you of any responsibility.

Are you willing to explore the reasons for your getting fired? Can you also read the indirect signals in a way that is truthful? Here are some crucial questions to answer.

Was Your Performance Inadequate? Were you fired because you weren't doing a job that could be done? Did your boss assess your lack of performance correctly? Were you not suited for this job all along, or did things just recently change? Have you been too ill to keep up the pace? Have there been diversions in your personal life that have consumed a lot of work time? Do you drink three beers or three shots of whiskey a day?

Was the Job Impossible? Were you fired because you were not able to do a job that could not be done by anyone, anyway? Did you choose not to read the early warning signals when they assigned you that impossible task, or didn't you realize it was impossible? Do you know what it is about you that allows you to get involved with impossible jobs? Did you know that people who undertake one impossible task usually undertake other impossible jobs? What other impossible jobs are you now involved with?

Did Your Performance Threaten Your Manager? Were you fired because you were doing a job that could be done? At first glance, this may seem like a silly question. More often than we'd like to believe, someone does a terrific job, makes somebody look bad because the job was done well, and gets fired for it. A variation on this theme happens when a person does a job well and becomes the target of destructive envy. This happens because some managers are so competitive that they are unable to tolerate high performance from their own employees. There are also those work groups that function at an expected (and accepted) low performance level. If one person in the group functions at a high level, that person ends up scapegoated because he or she is just too different. Were any of the above your circumstances? Before you answer yes, remember these are questions which are easy on you and hard on everyone else.

Were You Fired Because You Were Doing a Job That Nobody Believed Could Be Done? Sometimes there is no room for Wonderwoman or Superman in an organization. This is a very rare situation. Usually the person who can pull this off ends up the owner or president of some company (if not the one they are working in all ready). One variation of this that is more common, and very destructive to organizations, is the situation where a person uses valuable company resources to do a job that no one in the company wanted done. The problem here is an unauthorized change in direction. If a company condones this activity, it is undermining its own upper levels of management. Did this happen with you? Did you have a project that was supported by your boss but not by upper levels of management? Did you go off in new directions without first having formal authorization from all relevant levels of leadership?

Lastly, there are two additional points that need to be carefully considered. As long as you (secretly) depend on your ex-boss by blaming and focusing your rage at him or her, you keep yourself from making your own decisions. You run the dangerous risk of using your boss the way he or she might have used you: as a scapegoat that prevents you from dealing with the more important issues.

You need to spend some time struggling to get a picture that is bigger than just you and getting fired. What was going on in the company at the time? What were the economic forces impinging on your job? Remember how organizations work, how managers manage, how groups function. Knowing what the pressures were on your boss will alleviate your tendency to devalue yourself (things will be less personal when seen clearly) and get you to the work of surviving.

Now we go on to the practical behaviors you can use to deal with this nightmare.

DON'T BOW YOUR HEAD
IN SEVERANCE

Here are a series of firm suggestions to help you get what is fairly yours from your company as well as from yourself.

Know How to Use a Poker Face. Mask all of your bitterness. Go into all meetings very cool. Avoid any threatening behaviors on your part. They tend to create defensive behaviors, defensive formalities, and legalisms.

Be Prepared for an Inevitable Inundation of Documentation Against You. Your company may have all the operative and performance data, plus budget sheets, to justify firing you on the basis of the economy alone. They also may have literally hundreds of pieces of paper to justify firing you on the basis of your "poor" long-term performance and/or a single episode of misconduct. Being prepared means

knowing that this can happen and not allowing it to deter you from charting your own course of action toward a fair severance package. Being prepared also means being able to separate the facts of your career from fictions created by the company's need to move you out. Being prepared means being honest with yourself about what mistakes you did make so you don't end up being, or appearing, defensive around issues where you were in the wrong. The preparations I am talking about are as much emotional as factual.

Ask Firmly for Severance Pay. Establish quickly that you do not want your employer to fight with you over severance and other unemployment benefits.

Ask For Two Weeks Pay for Each Year You Were With the Company. Settle for one week's pay for each year you were with the company. This may sound like a game. It isn't. It's called bargaining and being treated with respect.

Collect on All Unused Time and Pay. Make unused vacation pay, overtime pay, unused sick time, and compensatory time clear entitlements.

Don't Hesitate to Call on Your Friends. Don't be afraid to use whatever sure friends you have in the company. Getting support from a major customer of the company and influential people in the community can be helpful. They can negotiate in your behalf very effectively if, and when, the circumstances seem appropriate to you.

Read Your Contract and the Company's Personnel Manual. See p. 183 earlier in this book for a discussion of this.

Consult a Good Tax Lawyer or Accountant. You will need help to figure out the best way to fit your severance package together with your pension plan. Compute the benefits you are entitled to under any pension or profit-sharing plan. Know your rights! They are protected by the Employment Retirement Income Security Act (ERISA) passed in 1974. Consider whether you should ask for a flat settlement, a fixed period of time on full salary while you conduct a job search, or a partial-pay contract.

A flat settlement is a one-step payment. It may be helpful to solve current financial dilemmas. Be careful of this. You are under stress, and those unpaid bills do cause a lot of pain. However, what will you do a little later on when the one payment is gone? Might it not be wiser to approach your creditors and arrange a payment schedule?

The partial-pay contract can offer you the administrative support of the company and freedom to make moves toward other jobs. This kind of contract essentially hires you as a part-time employee with full administrative support. In addition there may be important work that needs to be completed which will benefit your future career as well as your old company. Partial-pay contracts can be offered in lieu of outplacement services.

Read All Policy Statements of Your Medical Insurance. Ask your attorney or someone in the insurance business to help you translate them. Watch out for loss of major medical insurance. You might consider requesting a few extra days on the payroll to enable you to get floater coverage from your own insurance agent. Sometimes requesting an unpaid leave of absence as part of severance allows the corporate medical insurance coverage to continue uninterrupted.

Review Your Life and Disability Insurance. What policies are transferable over to you? When purchasing insurance, consider shopping for the least expensive insurance from a reputable company. There is no need to build cash value in an insurance policy at a time when you are needing liquidity for present day living. Inexpensive life and disability insurance will help diminish current apprehensions you may have about being able to provide for your family should your health be a problem.

How Much Time to Leave Do You Have? What would be the optimum time?

What is Available to Help You With Future Job Planning? Is there temporary office space and administrative support available? If the company does offer you secretarial support, don't forget to have friends call you at the office regularly. This is not an extreme suggestion. It will help you feel busy and in contact with the outside world. Your friends' calls will help you monitor any unconscious wishes on the part of the company to make your departure more uncomfortable than it already is.

If there is no support available, then hire an answering service to monitor your temporary office space (even if this ends up being your home phone). This will cost forty to sixty dollars per month and is well worth the expense. People will relate better to an answering service than to an answering machine (a distant second choice). If you leave your phone unanswered you may find yourself missing important calls. At the very least you may end up worrying unnecessarily about having missed calls. Some people without an answered phone find themselves unable to leave the house for fear of missing a call.

What Letters of Reference Will You Have Written? Who will sign them? Get a commitment in writing concerning your references. You should always have a current resume which clearly states your accomplishments. On the day you are fired it is fair to ask your boss to date and initial this resume until he or she writes you a more complete letter of reference. Consider writing your own letter of reference and have your boss sign it. Either simple act will allay a lot of your anxiety and pain. It will also serve to keep fresh in your ex-boss's mind just who should get credit for your accomplishments.

If your letter of reference arrives with gross inaccuracies, immediately confront its author. Tell the writer (do not ask) to do it right. Suggest firmly that you have met with your lawyer who is prepared to file suit against the boss and the company. This may sound drastic, but the price you will pay for allowing these matters to slip is potentially catastrophic. Treat this as a serious problem and act decisively. Search around in the company for people who are willing to write good letters of reference for you. Getting someone to do this is not only practical and helpful for future employment, it also does wonders for some of those acidic feelings inside of you. There will be a genuine decrease in your feelings that everyone in the company somehow betrayed you.

Be Sure You Have a Letter of Severance. This should document the date and time of your departure and the exact reasons for your leaving. Do not avoid this painful task. There is a difference between being laid-off, getting fired, and quitting when it comes to determining unemployment compensation.

Take All Your Ideas With You. The ones submitted to and developed by the company belong to the company. But having your own copies clearly establishes your participation. The undeveloped, unsubmitted ideas (done on your own time) belong to you. Do not leave copies of these behind.

Postpone Any Vacations. It is time to use your emergency financial plan. A vacation might feel terrific in the short haul, but the long-term consequences can be too painful.

What Will Be the Official Reason for Your Leaving? What is written in your personnel folder that might be used years from now for your references? How will the company publicly explain your termination? Will you get to approve any press releases? Should you hire a lawyer to help you think clearly?

What Can You Do About Any Noncompete Clauses in Your Contract? This is very complex. First of all, did you ever sign one? Many people do, but don't remember having ever done so (because they were so excited to get the job, and there were so many things to do in the personnel office the first day of the job). Do you have a copy of this document? Does this clause make you essentially unemployable in your field of expertise? If so, consider sitting down with your attorney and devising a strategy for renegotiating this clause. No matter how tight it may seem to you, remember your company wants to get rid of you (not the reverse), so use your leverage now.

Get a Physical Examination. You should have one if none has been done in the past six months. Be sure to discuss your firing with your doctor. Also ask for specific things you can do to reduce the immense stress you are under. Curtail caffeine, nicotine, and be certain to exercise forty-five minutes per day (after getting your doctor's approval). If you need to know where there are clinics that have sliding fee scales, then call the county medical society office and make the necessary inquiries.

Have Stationery Made Up. This is not just a veneer of professionalism; it is a clear signal to the world that you are functioning in your own best interest.

Collect Your Unemployment Insurance. Contain your feelings of shame and embarrassment about unemployment insurance. The Monthly Labor Review reported in March, 1983, that there were 13,346,000 people in this country who applied for, or renewed, their unemployment insurance in the first nine months of 1982. White collar unemployment was 5.0 percent in June of 1982, and was still rising. Everybody works hard for that insurance. It's there to be used.

When you go to the unemployment office, have with you your final termination notice and your social security card. At the unemployment office, you will register for your benefits and have an interview with a state employment service counselor. You will have to put up with supplying personal information and filling out forms. If you are eligible for unemployment insurance compensation, you will have a one to two week waiting period before you receive your first check. This waiting time can be longer, depending on bureaucratic delays. As soon as you start receiving money, you may have to report to the unemployment office each week. It isn't very pleasant because of the dehumanizing feelings all large bureaucracies create. However, you will see lots of other people using the system, the money will be helpful, and the negative part could motivate you in your push for new employment.

Have an Active Plan for Managing Your Money. There are time factors here that are difficult to anticipate. If you have a loan from the company's credit union, there is the possibility it may be deducted from your final paycheck. Review this with the credit union. Consider negotiating for a prolonged payback period as part of severance. It will be difficult to figure out how long you can expect to be unemployed. Employment experts advise clients to figure on being unemployed one month for each $10,000 in prior salary. Plan to cut back on your expenses. Here are some suggestions.

■ Review your entertainments. Look at what you "do" that has a ritualistic quality and compare the rituals to those things which are done for relaxation. Stop the "doings" and continue the "relaxers." This means you can probably stop all voluntary purchases (clothing, new appliances, or large gifts for others). Liquidate whatever membership assets you have in clubs by selling or stopping your memberships. Ask friends to take you as a guest (to continue future work contacts only). Eliminate any dues obligations. Remember, though, if the "relaxers" cost money, and you have been honest with your appraisal of their value, then in those cases spend the money!

■ Do not use credit cards. Avoid using checking accounts that have automatic loan guarantees.

■ Stop using alcohol and tobacco. There is a lot of money to be saved here and a lot of good health to be gained.

■ Read all the labels on items you might buy. This is true of all items, not just food. You will learn more about the product, and it will slow down any inclinations toward impulse buying. Reading forces you to hold the object in your hands long enough to decide if you really need it. This act may also teach you how much money you used to throw away.

■ Consider buying day-old food. There are many people in this country who take advantage of other people's preoccupation with perfect food by making these kinds of purchases. Purchase larger amounts of dairy products when you find a bargain. Did you know that most dairy products keep in refrigeration for a week or more after the last date of sale? Know where public food distribution sources are and what their distribution policies are. You may qualify.

■ Conserve energy. Consider selling one of your cars. (Doesn't every family have two these days?)

■ Consider using a religious institution near to you that offers financial and/or child care services.

Consider Finding a Mutual Support Group. There are other people in similar predicaments. You can advertise to find or begin a group in the personal section of your newspaper. It's best to have a leaderless group, without mental health people involved. Groups like this offer the opportunity to share anger and frustration openly. Ventilating these feelings in a safe place will go a long way toward taking the pressure off you and your family.

11

A BOUNCER
IN
SHARKSKIN
OUTPLACEMENT:
A HELPING HAND
FOR WHOSE BENEFIT?

E very organization has an administrative style. These styles are not to be equated with personalities, but they do set tones that characterize how people interact within companies. For example, in one company the only fair way to get vacation leave is to submit a formal request through formal channels. In another company the only fair way to get vacation leave is to discuss it with peers and arrange for coverage, then submit a notice of leaving and who is covering. In a third company, the fair way to go on vacation is to let the union representative negotiate time away. Every company has a different idea of what is "fair," or "good," or "honest," or "truthful," and that is its style. This part of the style is established by formal and informal administrative decree.

A corporate moral code, on the other hand, represents the cumulative experience of the company and all its individuals. Each person within the company has a distinct sense of morality, separate from the company. There is a constant, dynamic tension between the moral code of a company and the differing moral codes of all the individuals working in that company. This tension serves as a check and balance to any questionable moral code that can evolve in group settings.

So what does this have to do with a shaky job? Well, there are certain characteristics of corporate styles and morality that determine how the company defines "fairness" for those getting fired. Knowing these characteristics will help you chart your own course to a fair severance package.

THIS IS NO PILLOW FIGHT

Even if your organization has a reasonable or sensitive way of letting you go, it is not your needs they are trying to meet. The company is compelled to serve its own needs to survive, and firing is an event which can threaten the integrity of any organization. To avoid the threat, a company will soften the impact of letting an employee go for itself first and foremost. Even in the best of circumstances you should expect to be second in line for consideration and concern.

What was a mutually dependent and interactive relationship between you and your employer becomes potentially adversarial at the instant your job is in jeopardy. Getting pushed into the Termination Trap is an aggressive event, no matter how well the company cushioned the blow. As much as you may need to lean on someone, you also need to know whose helping hand is stretched out toward you. Somehow you have to know who that helping hand is intended to

help the most. Do not forget that. Yet, it is hard to think so clearly, let alone use whatever leverage you may have to help you when you are in a definite state of shock. Let's review some critical points to be cautious about.

A BOUNCER IN SHARKSKIN

They are called "outplacement experts." Just think for one minute what is hidden in that name. It's like our government changing the Secretary of War into the Secretary of Defense after World War II. How about cleaning up a garbageman into a trashman (trash is cleaner?), then into a refuse engineer, and lastly a sanitary engineer? In the mid-1970s the task of getting someone sacked, bounced, pink-slipped, or fired was changed into a "profession" called outplacement or de-cruitment. One fired executive described his company's outplacement expert as a deportation engineer. What these people do is help the firing company save money and feel less guilty about letting someone go. In a few cases outplacement consultation may help the company behave more humanely toward you during the firing procedure. Even if this happens, there is still something suspect here.

As the chairman of a large New York City outplacement firm, with several locations around the country and in Europe, said in a *New York Times* (March 18, 1979) article, "In blunt terms of dollars and cents, a well-structured termination can benefit a company significantly—certainly when measured against the costs of procrastination or some of the historically large lump payments or 'golden handshakes'."

According to one outplacement company's brochure, outplacement "can prevent the internal disruption and the torrents of negative publicity that more and more frequently accompany the rancorous, highly visible public firings that have hurt a number of prominent companies in recent months."

This is big business; an outplacement company usually charges your ex-employer from 10 to 15 percent of the fired person's annual salary, plus a flat fee for ancillary services supplied during the fired person's search for a new job.

Outplacement experts start out by working with and for the company that fired you. Though they end up working *with* you, they are still working *for* the company that let you go. They begin their consulting with the company by meeting with your boss and members of the personnel department and/or other managers within the company *before you are fired.* A fired employee can "bad-mouth the company." One of the major functions of outplacement companies is to reduce the negative feelings associated with being fired.

Remember this:
If you are ever fired,
find out to whom you are talking.
Write down everyone's name in the room.
Be sure to ask if they are executives
with the company or paid consultants.
You want to find out who is with you
at a time when you are so
psychologically vulnerable to
attitudinal manipulations.

Often the outplacement experts have collected very specific work and personal data on you before you were even fired. They know a lot more about you than you do about them. They may have discussed with your boss the best way to approach you about termination (an outplacement and CIA word). The expert may have helped your boss devise plausible reasons for telling you why you were fired. He or she may have helped soften the blow so your self-esteem would not go down and your rage would not go up. The outplacement expert will change your title from "employee" to "job candidate." Your new task will be to devise a marketing strategy for your skills. As one outplacement expert stated, "when a man gets fired, it isn't money he needs, it's dignity and professional help to do the one thing he was never trained to do—look for a job. We take a man and make him a professional at the art of job searching."

Brochures for prospective corporate clients often outline the process of outplacement. Usually there is a preliminary consultation with the fired individual, often immediately after getting fired, to help cope with the facts, including recognition of the corporation's interest in and concern for his or her successful re-employment/relocation. "Help" is offered during this stressful time on immediate problems such as how to tell the spouse, assess personal finances, and clarify the separation arrangements. Outplacement experts use many subtle techniques to position the fired employee away from angry feelings toward the company. This prevents common serious mistakes such as 'bad-mouthing' the company with other employees as well as outsiders, making premature future job contacts, and creating unnecessary concern in the family. All the while there are overtures to building the fired person's morale, plans of action developed, *including acceptance of the outplacement expert's approach to the dilemma* (maximizing the firing company's position).

In a personal interview, a vice president of one company informed me that "there is no confusion in our mind about who we are working for . . . the corporations. If someone walks in off the street and asks for our services on an individual basis, we politely inform them they have to go elsewhere. We have the reputation for working for the corporations' best interests and we don't want to confuse our image."

Some of the service consists of reviewing your personal goals, as well as your strengths and weaknesses in accomplishing those goals. If you choose to remain in the same field, it will be suggested that you explore self-employment and consultation work. They will recommend contacting industry-specialized search agencies, professional associations, and want ads of trade journals and business publications. You will be directed toward accumulating your own information on prospective employers. The good outplacement companies have specialized data bases targeted to your field. However, you will be expected to utilize library searches, chambers of commerce, specialized phone books, and industry publications to acquire this information. It will be suggested to you to contact church and social clubs, fraternal and professional societies, college friends, and business contacts. There should be help in writing a well-structured introductory letter and a resume that has a brief "scan time" (less than 30 seconds). Your interview techniques should be reviewed, preferably with video equipment so you can see for yourself what image you project. Another service offered is reviewing the details of negotiating for a new job: responsibility, job title, salary, relocation expenses, vacation, bonuses, and other work-related issues.

Being paid by your ex-company, this expert has to have the ability to serve two conflicting forces. You should know that from the very beginning. Remember that if the expert does a good job, he or she gets rehired by the company that fired you. But, does your ex-company ever come to you to see if the outplacement expert is doing a good job? While I was at one out-placement office, I was told that they kept no follow-up data on any of their individual clients because they measured satisfaction on the basis of how happy their corporate clients were with the services provided. At least with this company it was very clear in their minds just whose interests they were serving.

You don't have to accept these services. In fact, you may be able to negotiate for the $1,000 to $10,000 fee that would be paid to the outplacement service to use for yourself. Here are some things to do to cope with the subtle emotional pressures of the conflicting messages that come from outplacement.

■ Buy a copy of Richard Bolles' book, *What Color is Your Parachute?* This is a clearly written review of how to get a job. Geared mainly for recent graduates, it is still filled with practical suggestions about getting work and coping and changing. At least skim it, and then decide if you need an outplacement expert to hold your hand. Maybe family and friends can be equally helpful.

■ You have got to remember who pays the outplacement expert and ask yourself just what makes them so valuable to the company that fired you. Remember that this outplacement expert most probably consulted with your company prior to your getting fired. This person may have even helped plan the setting of your Termination Trap. Lastly, outplacement has a goal to work with your company to make firing you cost effective (despite their lucrative fee). It is possible you might benefit from the service, but be wary of accepting it when you are under so much personal distress.

■ Consider that the people who will be interacting with you on the day you are fired might have no formal clinical training in human vulnerabilities and reactions to stress. One outplacement executive told me that, "All of our specialists are ex-business people like myself; many of us have even been through being let go." There was even the openly stated implication in our interview that the "experts" gained their "expertise" from being fired from a previous job. This kind of expertise is worth about as much as a surgeon's claiming expertise in cardiac surgery because he had his own heart operated on.

■ Know the outplacement company that is being offered to you. Immediate involvement with outplacement at a time when you are so vulnerable can be very risky. Even the most accepted and successful outplacement service companies have severe ethical conflicts inherent in their being of help to you. They are paid by the company that fired you; their evaluation of you and your abilities is based on data from your ex-boss. They have to be doing something that pleases their boss (your ex-boss). In many respects that's all right, but you need to know what they do, who does it, how they do it, and what their results have been. Of course, the services will have all sorts of data extolling their own virtues. But this is your life they are "deporting," and their method of data collection has to be seriously biased. The only reasonable source of information concerning how valuable a particular outplacement service has been (and *might* be) is its past clients.

■ Have the company that wants to deport you introduce you to at least one of its ex-clients who is not employed by the outplacement company.

Any company that will not offer you this opportunity is, in fact, hiding something. Of course they can plead confidentiality, but don't buy it. Even in the field of medicine, when a person is confronted with going through a controversial, painful, or radical surgical procedure, it is standard procedure to have the patient meet with a person who has undergone the procedure. In addition, the physician is obligated to inform the person of the risks involved with the procedure.

■ Since your life is at stake in more ways than one, be certain to have the outplacement firm offer you the chance to meet alone with this ex-client. You must ask a lot of questions in a brief period of time. Here's how to do it. Remember to take copious notes. These notes may be useful to you later if you elect to accept the services and things don't go too well.

First, take the brochure from the outplacement company and ask about every service described: was it done, who did it and what was that person like, how was it done, and how successful was each service. Inquire about services provided that are not in the brochure. Be very diplomatic, but press for specific answers about inadequacies and failures. Be sure to get them.

Ask very detailed questions about the teaching techniques this company uses. Some outplacement companies use video equipment to give feedback on your job interviewing skills. The feedback can be done in different ways, but it should be done by someone with expertise in helping others learn how to change their behaviors.

You want to avoid further erosion of your self-esteem. On the other hand, learning about your deficiencies at a vulnerable time may make you more open to change. Do they have support groups where peers confront each other about behaviors? If so, what is the training and experience level of the group leaders? (Ask to see their resumes!) If the confrontation is done only by the staff, what techniques do they use? Is there videotaping? Companies that do outplacement often use confrontation as a tool. But confrontation for its own sake, or confrontation done by someone poorly skilled in interpersonal and emotional dynamics, can be a weapon. Remember, anything that has the potential to be beneficial, also has the possibility for harm.

If the outplacement service refuses to comply with your request to meet with an ex-client, consider that they are hiding something (like unethical conduct or failure), or they don't have follow-up information on their clients. A lack of follow-up may indicate an unwillingness to look at the quality of their own services. It also may indicate a pessimism about the service in general. For example, for years the federal government was involved with a form of outplacement service. People who were abusing heroin were sent to Lexington, Kentucky, for inpatient treatment of drug abuse. While the abusers were placed out there, the statistics on the numbers abusing heroin showed dramatic improvement. Long-term follow-up of discharged addicts done much later showed, however, that 95 percent went back to heroin. This data, acquired after years of sending people to Lexington, contributed to a major change in how drug addicts were, and are, treated. You need that long-term data to determine just how worthwhile the service is that's being offered to you.

■ Visit the outplacement facility. You can't expect to make a complete judgment just by visiting, but there is a better opportunity to feel the situation out if you are there.

■ The most important thing to remember is that even those companies that have been successful in outplacement work have to teach values that enhance their clients' abilities to get new jobs. These values may be stressfully different from your own. Do you feel strong enough to hang on to your own values? Think carefully about this.

Consider, also, how you will feel about a new job, several months later, that was found (indirectly) by your ex-boss. Will you feel that you never made a clean break? Or that you have to "prove" your worth to your new boss because of the connection to your previous employer? It may be much more worthwhile to conduct your job-search privately, leaving those old feelings behind.

The point here is to be very careful of accepting any help from strangers. (Sound familiar?) Your coping *must* be oriented toward serving you, and you alone. *The day you are fired can be too confusing and too jumbled to leave yourself open to the direct and intentional manipulation of your feelings and plans by someone who has been hired by your ex-boss.*

12

LIFE AFTER
JOB LOSS
A REVIEW

T his is a brief review of useful activities more thoroughly discussed earlier. It is also a quick benediction for a quality work-life. If you've read this far, it's because there are, or may be, serious work problems in your life. Start to work on these problems now!

■ Now is the time to treat yourself as indispensable to your own well-being. There has never been a better time than now to start exercising, stop smoking, and change your eating habits.

■ Cherish your personal life. You need to work hard to respect yourself. It won't hurt to have family and friends on your side. Keep working in this area. Consider your close relationships to be the center of your support systems.

Allow for open, unstructured time to talk, face to face, candidly, seriously, and deeply with your spouse or close friend. Expect and accept anger, tension, and fear without surprise, shock, or withdrawal. Acknowledge and reward all expressions of feeling in your close relationship, and expect the same in return. This will help you build a useful support system for the future.

■ Keep your Type A traits carefully in check. Keep working to develop a more relaxed, assured attitude to your present life. Review chapter 7.

■ Read that running account of yourself you made earlier. If it doesn't exist yet, then return to chapter 7 and do it right now.

■ Review the up-to-date assessment of your job requirements.

■ Stay in contact with your confidant.

■ Watch your alcohol and drug consumption. Now, more than ever, you need a clear head.

■ Good luck (we all need that).

I WISH YOU
LOTS OF SKILL

READING LIST

Argyris, C. **Integrating the Individual and the Organization.** New York: John Wiley & Sons, 1964.

Argyris, C. **Personality and Organization.** New York: Harper, 1957.

Bennis, W. G. "Leadership Theory and Administrative Behavior: The Problem of Authority." **Administration Science Quarterly** 4 (1959): 299.

Berne, E. **Games People Play.** New York: Grove Press, 1967.

Bion, W. R. **Experiences in Groups.** New York: Basic Books, 1961.

Coulson, R. **The Termination Handbook.** New York: The Free Press, Div. of MacMillan Publishing Company, 1981.

Department of Health, Education and Welfare. **Work in America: Report of a Special Task Force to the Secretary of Health, Education and Welfare.** Cambridge: The M.I.T. Press, 1980.

Drucker, P. F. **The Concept of the Corporation.** New York: New American Library, 1964.

Golding, W. **Lord of the Flies.** New York: G. P. Putnam's Sons, 1964.

Group for the Advancement of Psychiatry. **Job Loss—A Psychiatric Perspective.** New York: Mental Health Materials Center, 1982.

Hall, E. T. **The Hidden Dimension.** Garden City, N.Y.: Doubleday & Co., Inc., 1966.

Hall, E. T. **The Silent Language.** Garden City, N.Y.: Doubleday & Co., Inc., 1959.

Hymowitz, C. "Managers' Malaise: Fear of Unemployment Takes Emotional Toll At White Collar Levels." **The Wall Street Journal,** 19 July, 1982.

LeBon, G. **The Crowd.** New York: The Viking Press, 1967.

Levine, R. **Culture, Behavior, and Personality.** Chicago: Aldine Publishing Co., 1973.

Little, C. B. "Technical-Profession Unemployment: Middle-Class Adaptability to Personal Crisis." **Sociological Quarterly** 17 (1976): 262–274.

McGregor, D. **Leadership and Motivation.** Cambridge: The M.I.T. Press, 1966.

Miller, E. J. and Rice, A. K. **Systems of Organization.** London: Tavistock Publications, 1967.

Miller, J. "New Prestige For Those in the Firing Trade." **The New York Times,** 18 March, 1979.

Rice, A. K. **Learning for Leadership.** London: Tavistock Publications, 1963.

Roethlisberger, F. J. and Dickson, N. J. **Management and the Work.** New York: John Wiley & Sons, Inc., 1967.

Ruesch J. **Therapeutic Communication.** New York: W. N. Norton & Co., 1961.

Runde, R. "What To Do If You Lose Your Job." **Money,** 11 (1982):109–122.

Sennett, R. **Authority.** New York: Alfred A. Knopf, 1980.

Simmons, J. & Mares, W. **Working Together.** New York: Alfred A. Knopf, 1983.

Sumner, W. G. **Folkways.** New York: Dover Publications, Inc., 1959.

Terkel, S. **Working.** New York: Avon Books, 1975.

Verba, S. **Small Groups and Political Behavior—A Study of Leadership.** New Jersey: Princeton University Press, 1972.

vonBertalanffy, L. **General System Theory.** New York: George Braziller, 1968.

White, J. S. "Today's Focus: You're Fired! Thank you!" New York: The Associated Press, November 6, 1978.